Y0-BQT-152
NO LONGER PROPERTY OF
FULLERTON PUBLIC LIBRARY

Matchbox Labels

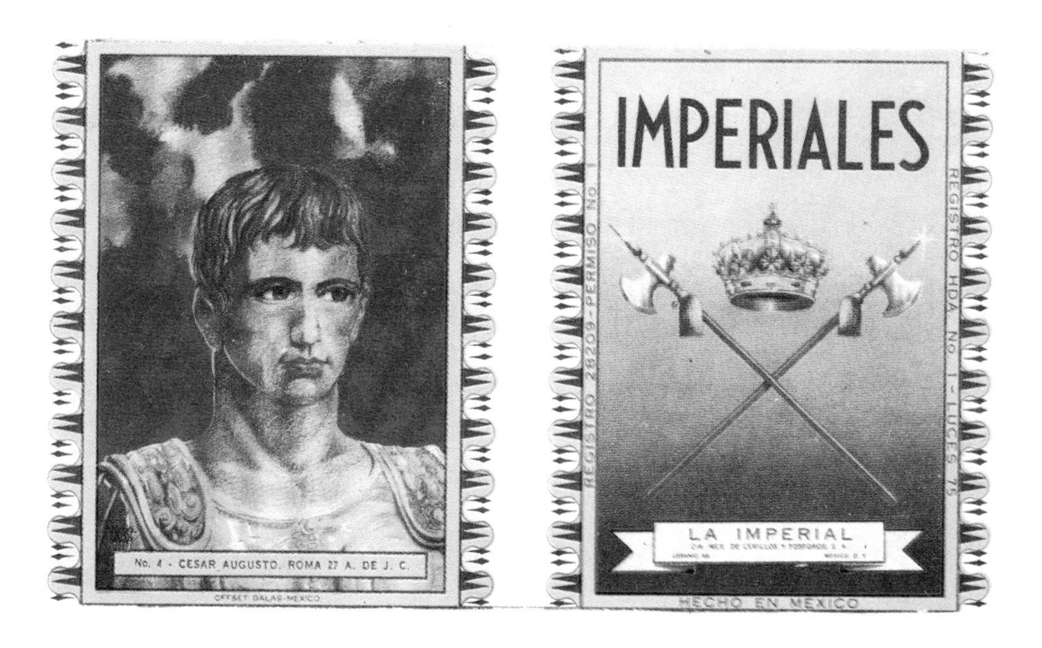

OTHER BOOKS BY THE SAME AUTHOR

Collecting Matchbox Labels

Flower Arrangement with a Marine Theme

MATCHBOX LABELS

Joan Rendell

741.694
REN

FREDERICK A. PRAEGER, *Publishers*
New York · Washington

FULLERTON PUBLIC LIBRARY
FULLERTON, CALIFORNIA

741.694
REN

BOOKS THAT MATTER

Published in the United States of America in 1968
by Frederick A. Praeger, Inc., Publishers
111 Fourth Avenue, New York, N.Y. 10003

© 1968 in London, England, by Joan Rendell

All rights reserved

Library of Congress Catalog Card Number: 68-26676

Printed in Great Britain

Contents

1. Swedish label issued by Jönköping, 1890, for the USA market 2. From Iceland, the Great Geyser 3. The Shah of Persia, one of set of 4 issued on his coronation on 26.10.67 4. St Basil's Cathedral, Moscow, on a Czechoslovakian label 5. Regional costume from Turkey 6. The Victoria Cross, instituted in 1856, honoured by Belgium 7. From set of Belgian labels on sale in Britain late 1960s 8. Ten labels from Portugal featured sports 9. For use in new territory taken over by Indonesia 1963 10. First label of the Fiji Match Factory, 1963 11 & 12. Midget labels from Iran

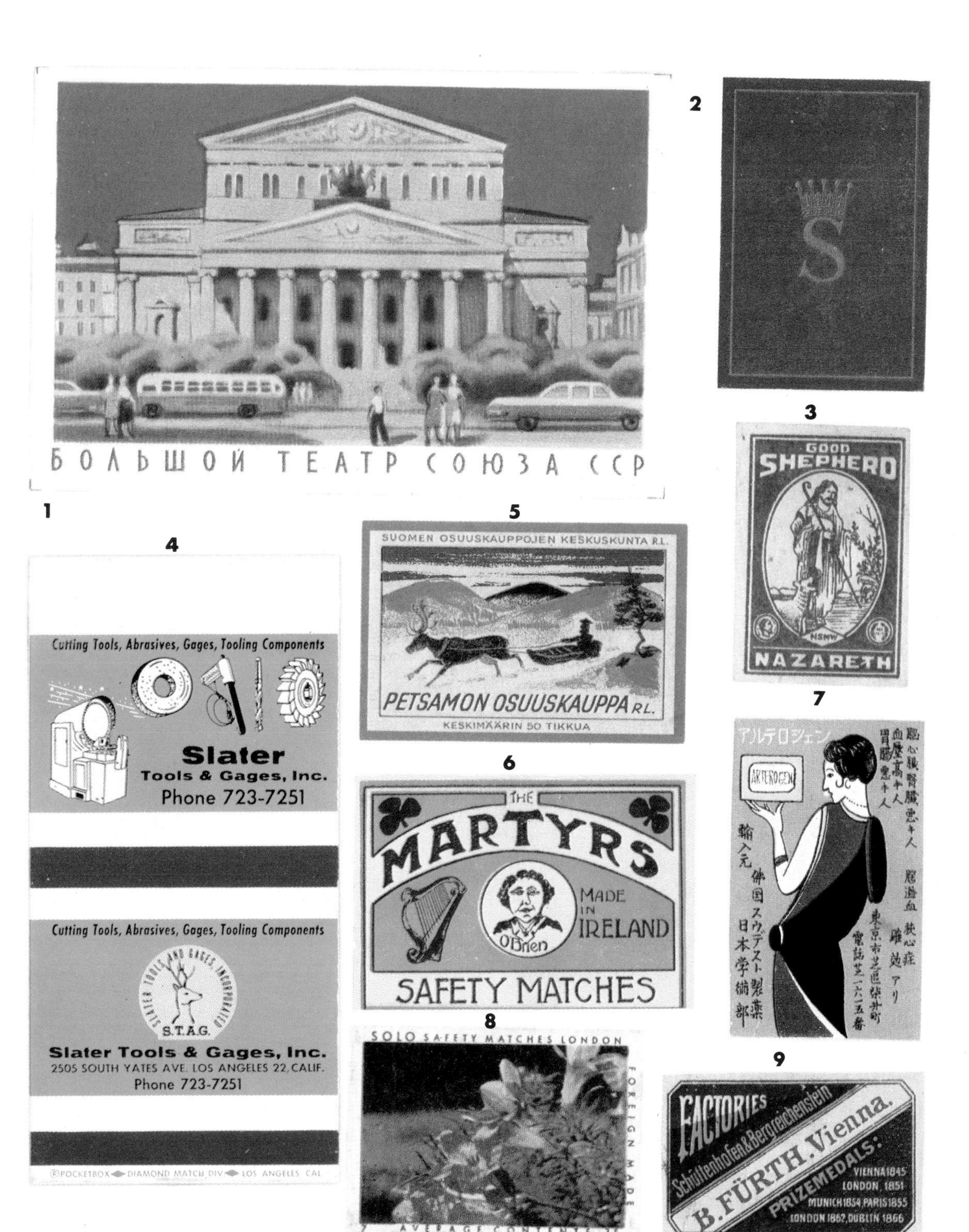

1. The Bolshoi Theatre on a label for large-size Russian box 2. Personal label of Queen Sybilla of Sweden 3. Rare Indian religious label 4. Modern US advertising skillet 5. Finnish label for use in Lapland 6. From set of 4 Irish martyrs 7. Japanese advertising label of the 1930s 8. Austrian label, one of a set for matches sold in Britain c1959 9. Old Austrian label

1

2

3

4

5

6

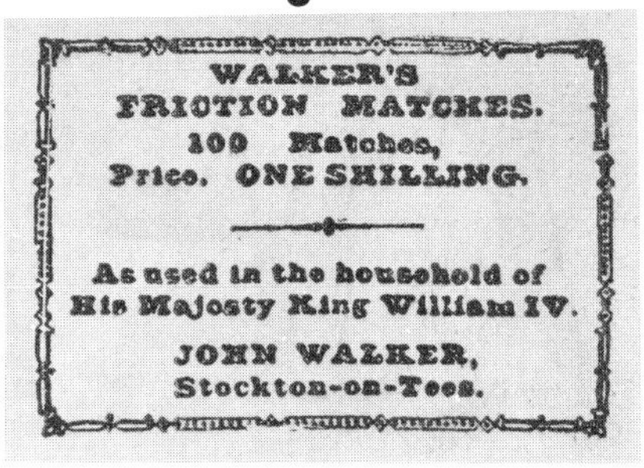

WALKER'S
FRICTION MATCHES.
100 Matches,
Price. ONE SHILLING.

As used in the household of
His Majesty King William IV.

JOHN WALKER,
Stockton-on-Tees.

7

8

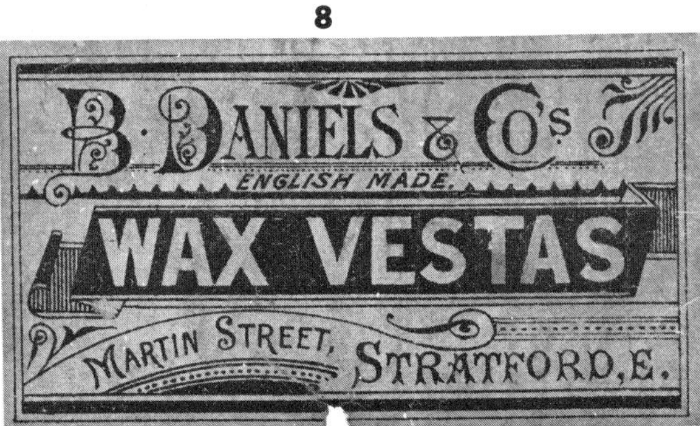

1. Old British label for matches with stems braided with cotton 2. Early safety match made in Austria-Hungary, 1870, by Fl Pojatzi & Co for Bulgaria 3, 4 & 5. Three early pillbox labels 6. Facsimile print of the first-ever label on a box of friction matches, 1827 7. Congreves were in use long before safety matches 8. Early British label from a firm long defunct

1 *The History of Labels*

SCRAPS OF coloured paper or miniature works of art? Whichever way one regards matchbox labels, they have a certain fascination which cannot be denied; for colour, variety and as a window on the world, few simple things of everyday life can offer more than the ubiquitous matchbox.

Perhaps part of the fascination lies in the fact that they do not follow any set pattern. Designs can be as whimsical as a manufacturer wishes, or they can be planned and selected with a keen eye for the market in which they are to be sold. But if the manufacturer relies more on his name than on a fancy design for his boxes or if he is singularly lacking in imagination, then the labels can be dull and wordy and little else.

Pictorial matchbox labels are now taken for granted, but this was not always the case. When Stockton-on-Tees chemist John Walker invented the friction match in 1826, he was concerned only that the public should know what his invention was and how to use it. So the first-ever matchbox label—for Walker's 'Friction Lights' —was a small white piece of paper with black lettering which mildly boosted the product and gave careful instructions for its use. High-power advertising did not exist in those days and no one found anything wrong with Walker's label; it served its purpose and that was all that mattered. Walker did not in fact provide a label at all for his matches until at least two years after he invented them and first put them on the market.

But in 1830 N. Jones & Co (one of the firms which had quickly produced a slight variation on Walker's invention) made history by sticking on its boxes of 'Royal Patent Lucifers' a pale-green label with a crudely-printed design of an Englishman and a Highlander smoking, two serpents breathing flames adding extra decoration. The Royal Arms adorned the centre. This is generally accepted as the first pictorial label and certainly no earlier claimant has ever come forward.

Even then no one saw a great future for the purely pictorial label and in those pedantic times an elaborately-written script and swirls of lines were thought of more highly, so that for some years after Jones's bold experiment really pictorial labels were not produced and the labels for the early boxes of Lucifers and Congreves were printed in genteel black on white paper, with designs of geometric lines framing the title and sometimes instructions on how the contents of the box should be used.

From these chaste beginnings the often flamboyant labels of today derived. Early manufacturers experimented with pictorial labels, found they proved popular and went from strength to strength. By 1880 labels had become so colourful that people were collecting them. The best at this time were produced on the Continent, and Italy, Belgium, Spain, Austria, and other countries vied to produce the finest examples.

Nowadays it would be difficult to say which countries issue the best specimens. Mexico probably held the palm in the late 1930s and even until the late 1950s, but the quality of its labels seems to have deteriorated since then. Sweden, Switzerland and Italy also produce some magnificent examples today, mainly for large 'drawing-room' or 'household' boxes. Argentina is catching up fast in this way with some beautifully-printed sets of large-size labels depicting military uniforms, etc, but such products are only for its home market. The USSR also issues some very fine glazed labels in sets for the tourist trade and, unlike in Argentina, these are not generally available for home consumption; local purchasers, although not entirely banned, are discouraged from buying the 'gift' boxes shown with such enthusiasm to foreign visitors.

It would be impossible to list in this or any

1

2

3

4

5

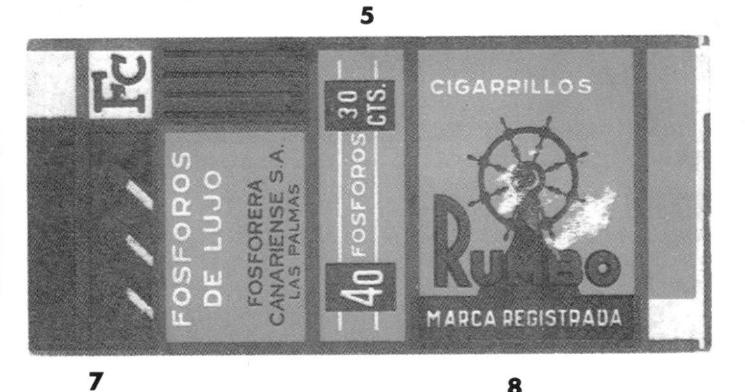

6

7

8

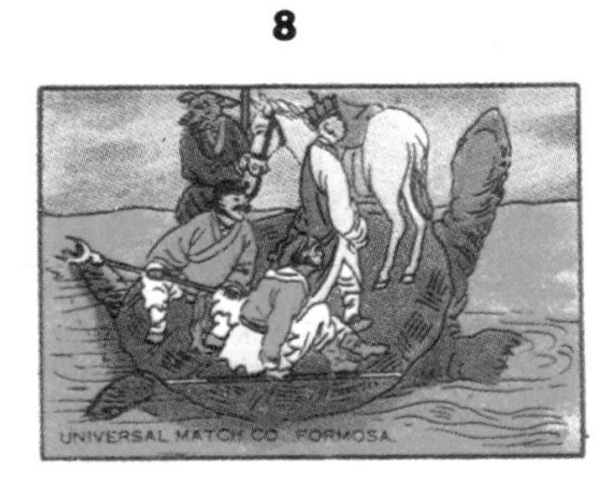

1. From the set of 8 handsome labels showing Australian aboriginal bark paintings, 1966 2. Coronation commemorative, New Zealand 3. Modern Japanese advertising label 4. Pre-1939 Esthonian label 5. All-round label from the Canary Islands 6. Very rare Albanian label printed on scrap paper, 1956-7 7. From a popular set of 6 Italian export labels, 1940s 8. From set of 20 fairytale labels from Taiwan

1. From rare set of 1930s labels from USA 2. Unusual Indian design 3. Old Eirrean label 4. Dramatic Finnish label, now scarce, for export to Iceland 5. Distinguished old glazed German label 6. Miniature box from Macao 7. A view from India 8. Old Norwegian label 9. Modern Israeli label 10. US State label of the 1930s 11. From a popular set of modern Russian export labels showing every quarter-hour round the clock

other volume *all* the subjects which have been portrayed on matchbox labels or on skillet-type matchboxes (where the design is printed straight on the cardboard outer cover of the box). Likewise it is almost impossible to name anything which has *not*, at some time or another, appeared on a matchbox: birds to bombs, cats to cathedrals, dogs to decorations—all can be found. The number of people in the world who collect matchbox labels has risen steadily over the years and there are now many thousands. The British Matchbox Label & Booklet Society has had well over 2,000 members passing through its ranks since it was founded in 1945.

Many brands which present a probably colourful and off-beat picture are unnamed, and the reason for this is usually that they are destined for a market where a large proportion of the would-be purchasers is illiterate or semi-literate, and a picture therefore conveys a great deal more than a fancy name. Early Japanese labels are noteworthy in this respect. Many hundreds of charming designs were produced, often with, to the Western mind, inexplicable associations in the designs, and untitled. The manufacturers were well aware that the vast majority of their customers were unlikely to ask for any brand of matches by name, whereas something which aroused interest or curiosity in picture form would sell readily.

2 Animals and Birds

Animals and birds have always been popular subjects for labels; in fact, they form the largest group of subjects chosen. An animal or bird in a play will usually steal the scene and it will serve the same purpose on a matchbox label. In fact, one Italian manufacturer was said to have commented some years ago that his firm's labels which depicted living things from spiders to elephants were selling so well that he intended in future to concentrate on brands named after and labelled with animals, birds and insects. It was noticeable that for some time that particular firm

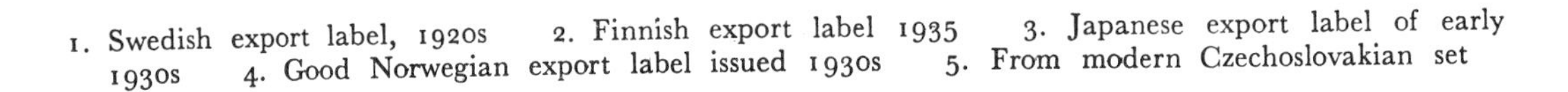
1. Swedish export label, 1920s 2. Finnish export label 1935 3. Japanese export label of early 1930s 4. Good Norwegian export label issued 1930s 5. From modern Czechoslovakian set

1. For wax matches sold in Colombia, Central America 2. Italian export brand 3. Belgian export brand, 1920s 4. One of South Africa's most popular brands 5. Scarce old Irish label 6. Modern label from Malaya before the formation of Malaysia 7. Recent issue, one of a set, from Communist China 8 & 9. The distinctive shape of labels from Mauritius 10. Italian export brand from SAFFA, Milan

1

2

3

5

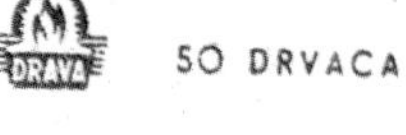

6

4

9

7

8

10

11

1. Delightfully-coloured modern Hungarian label, one of a set of 16 for 'club' boxes 2. Popular Australian brand 3. Czechoslovakian export label 4. American product for sale in North America 5. Swedish export label of the 1920s 6. From a set of modern labels from Yugoslavia 7. Finnish export label of the period between the wars 8 & 10. Indian labels overprinted after price changes after world war II 9. Colourful Dutch export label of the 1920s 11. Old Belgian export label

did issue a great many single labels, each one showing a different representative of the world's fauna.

Really old labels seldom featured animals or birds in their designs. Such things were not considered sufficiently dignified by the manufacturers of the early nineteenth century; royalty and important personages or buildings were more to their liking. Towards the end of the century however ideas changed, and the flood of animal labels commenced. Between the two world wars Great Britain imported about 50 per cent of its matches from the Continent of Europe and this period was the heyday of animal and bird designs, Belgium being particularly fond of them as designs for match brands.

Many collectors of matchbox labels organise their collections on a thematic or subject basis and animals and birds are one of the most popular subjects, the scope being so great. No particular animal or bird can be pinpointed as the favourite. Lions and tigers are featured frequently, with perhaps dogs and elephants sharing second place and cats coming in third, but one can find almost any creature.

Japan has probably issued more labels depicting animals and/or birds than any other country and very often, particularly in the period around 1880 to 1930, the creatures were shown acting as humans. For instance, a mouse draws a handcart in which sits a large cat holding an open parasol over its head; two monkeys dance together to the music of an instrument played by another monkey; a man converses with a frog; two cats sit writing at a table. All these rather curious labels were untitled but presumably their message was clear to the Oriental mind, for they were for home sale only. The majority were well-drawn and printed in soft colours and must have been produced in great quantity, as vast numbers have survived to this day and they are represented in most collections. Many were included in albums of labels made up specially for sale to seafaring men, who bought them eagerly as unusual souvenirs of the Far East.

Nowadays the fashion is for sets of labels, popular for two reasons. Sets are welcomed by collectors because they provide excitement and interest in the chase for completion and thus

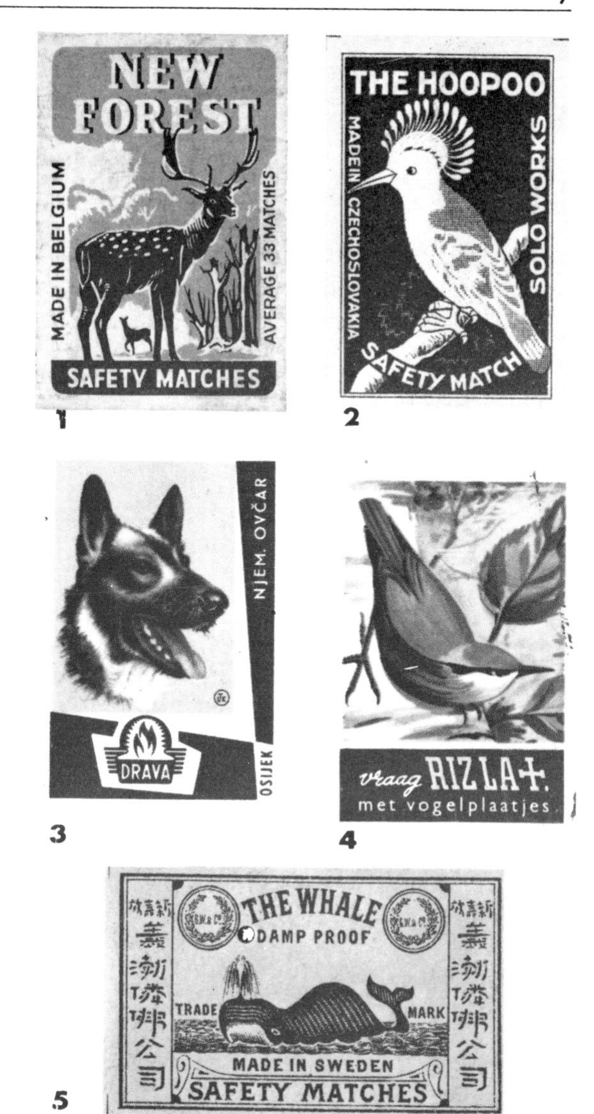

1. Belgian export label, 1940-50 2. A not very realistic hoopoe from Czechoslovakia 3. From a modern Yugoslavian set of 12 dogs 4. Nuthatch from a set of 40 labels from Holland issued early 1960s 5. Pre-world war I label from Sweden

create an incentive to collecting. And the manufacturers, because of the demand for their products by collectors, enjoy increased business. Not surprisingly, among the most popular subjects selected for sets in many parts of the world are animals and birds. A modern Australian set

1. Canadian skillet of 1930s, showing prairie hen or Bob White 2. British Guianan label of 1930s
3. Modern label from Communist China 4. World war II label issued in Thailand showing Siamese white elephant

showing examples of the country's fauna was a 'sell-out' to collectors anxious to gather the 64 different designs before they went off the market, and similar stories could be told of sets from Holland, Hungary, Yugoslavia, Czechoslovakia, Russia, etc, the sets varying in length from 10 to over 50.

Both Hungary and the USSR have in recent years used birds on labels to adorn large-size 'club' boxes, and both have employed vastly different styles in which to portray them. Hungary's set of 16 labels shows birds in natural colours against a background of their natural habitat—a delightful set. Russia, on the other hand, has chosen to make its bird a stylised modern version and the difference is very marked when the two labels are seen together, as in the illustration. Both have beauty in their own way, both are well printed and finished.

That Antipodean curiosity the platypus, more commonly known as the Australian duckbill and found nowhere else in the world, appeared on an Australian label of the year 1911 and a Belgian manufacturer of the early 1900s even depicted 'The Antediluvian Iguanadon', the genus of extinct gigantic lizards which included the dinosaur.

That one was not a best seller—no one could get round the tongue-twisting brand name!

Indian labels feature animals to a great extent, and usually ferocious ones. The tiger is naturally popular; lions, cheetahs and gorillas have appeared on many Indian labels, elephants, horses and foxes are also common. Often the drawings bear little resemblance to the real animal, but the brand name dispels any doubt. Match manufacturing in India is largely a business outlet for the 'small man' and matches are made and boxes labelled in incredibly primitive

1. Film dog Rin Tin Tin on a colourful Mexican label 2. Russian space dog Laika 3. Early Dutch label for export to Scandinavia 4. Russian export label c1934 5 & 6. Italian export labels issued immediately after world war II 7. The world's most tongue-twisting brand-name 8. Russian export label c1923

1

2

1. The 'king-size' label from a modern Russian set of 18 ordinary-size boxes and one 'club'-size box 2. Norwegian export label of the 1920s

conditions. The large Western India Match Co (WIMCO) turns out to a different type of product altogether, of course, and some of its labels are most artistic. But particularly in South India the 'cottage industry' in matchmaking flourishes and it is these tiny concerns which sometimes produce such extraordinary pictures.

Communist China has made the most of its famous panda and since the species has become more or less a symbol of China it has been featured on several very attractive labels. The subject is a 'natural'—appealing, unusual in colouring and unmistakably Chinese. Incidentally, it was not until 1957 that sets of labels were ever issued in China. Pre-1939 Chinese labels featured the bat and the deer to a large extent, both these creatures being regarded as symbols of longevity.

It is interesting to note how countries often feature the animals indigenous to them. For instance, a USA label of the 1940s was entitled 'Wolverine' and showed the head of the small North American carnivorous animal of that name. The South African Springboks rugby team is famous; not so well-known is the South African matchbox label 'Springbok' which shows, jumping over the rising sun, the graceful South African gazelle which leaps so high in play or when alarmed. The now defunct Tafelburg Match Co of South Africa, which opened in 1948 and closed in 1951, issued an all-round-the-box label entitled 'Koodoo' with a lifelike drawing of the South African antelope so named. Switzerland has shown a St Bernard dog and a chamois; Thailand exported matches with labels showing one of its famous 'white' elephants. Trinidad had 'Magpie' brand in the 1930s; Finland gave us 'Rendier' (sic).

One of the nicest series of labels featuring animals and birds was the 'Fauna Iberica' set issued in Spain for several years from 1950 onwards. These all-round labels came in an almost unending succession of permutations, with a picture on both front and back of the box, the soft natural colours making them a most desirable collectors' item. They were sold mainly in southern Spain and in 1951 were very elusive. It was in that year that one collector-tourist almost sparked off an international incident by trying to retrieve a scarce box which had been deposited in no-man's-land at the Spanish-French frontier. These labels were scarce for some time and probably unique in that wild stories began to circulate suggesting that they were used for conveying secret messages; that the endless permutations of pictures had special significance etc. It was never discovered where these rumours started and they were, of course, entirely without foundation. It may even have been a smart advertising stunt to

1. Australian label, 1911 2. Pre-1939 label from Trinidad 3. Modern Indian label 4. Rare modern label from Assam 5. From box bought in South Korea during the war, 1950 6. Modern label from Macao, Portuguese possession in China

sell the matches!

Over the years some famous animals have been pictured on matchbox labels. Notable among these is Laika, the first Sputnik dog, featured very realistically on Russian labels for boxes for the home market at the time of her ill-fated journey into space. Canine film stars Rin Tin Tin and Lassie have both given their names to match brands and have been portrayed on the labels—'Rinty' in Mexico and Lassie in Belgium. In the realms of film fantasy two other famous 'animals' have been so honoured—Felix the cartoon cat and King Kong.

Various factors of course assist the choice of animal or bird: consideration of the market for which the label is destined; perhaps the possibility of a play on the match manufacturer's name; the availability of ready-made trade mark if some particular creature is associated with the country of origin (such as the platypus in Australia); or, and this seems to be the usual criterion, the personal preference of the manufacturer or label designer. In the latter context the search is for originality, and in the 1940s 'La Imperial' all-round-the-box labels from Mexico carried on their reverse sides a series of pictures of prehistoric animals, reptiles and fish; an interesting departure, for that country, from the more usual dogs, bulls or scenes from the bullfight.

The range of birds depicted on labels is almost as great as that of animals. A Canadian skillet for a large-size box scored in originality by depicting a pair of prairie hens (known as Bob Whites), a design not duplicated by the other country, and a Belgian manufacturer of the 1920s cashed in on the popularity of canaries as cage birds by issuing the 'Best Canary Safety Match' with a drawing of the bird on the label, although it is not identifiable as any particular breed! Probably because the kingfisher is colourful a Dutch manufacturer of the same period adorned a matchbox with it and although it is actually printed in only three colours on white paper, clever blending and overprinting produced a remarkably natural-looking bird and an eye-catching label.

Some years ago the Elkayes Match Factory in the then Federated Malay States issued several labels with the prefix 'golden' in the title and 'Golden Parrot' is one of these, although it actually shows a bright yellow cockatoo dram-

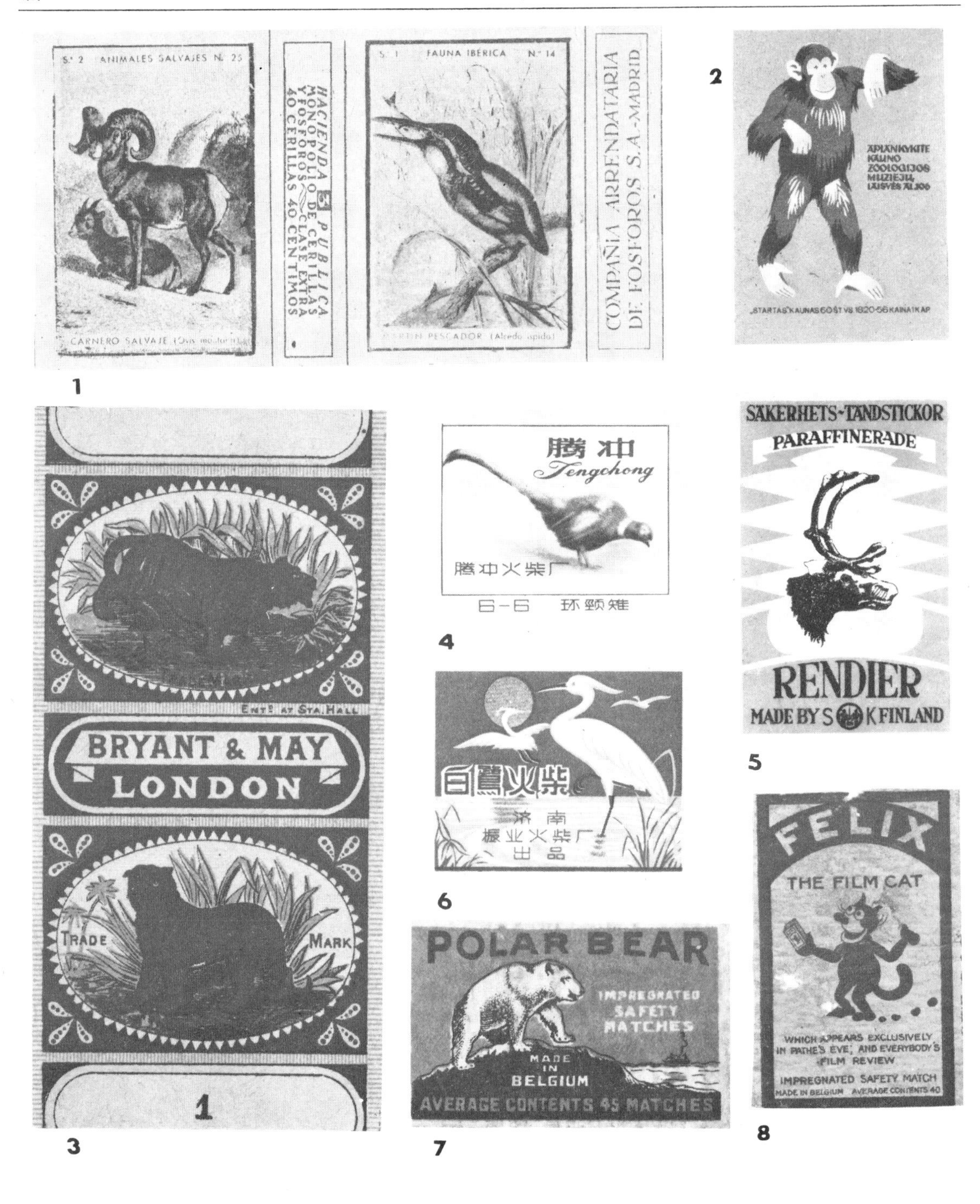

1. One of the controversial Spanish 'Fauna Iberica' set 2. Recent Russian label from a set for the home market 3. Early British label—a brand still on the market 4 & 6. Two of recent set from Communist China 5. Pre-1939 Finnish label 7. Belgian export label of the early 1930s 8 Belgian label showing a popular film cartoon figure of the 1920s

1 Issued in Sweden pre-1939 2. One of the first labels issued in Nigeria 3. One of modern Belgian set 4. Pre-1939 Czechoslovakian label 5. Modern export label from Poland 6. Modern Portuguese label for the home market

atically set against a black background. Czechoslovakia produced 'The Hoopoo', and not only the spelling but the fact that the design was printed entirely in blue on white paper were points to dismay ornithologists. It was destined for the Solo Works' North African market, but all its wording is in English.

Some years ago British Guiana issued a label entitled 'The Toucan' at the time when a famous British brewery company was prominently featuring that bird in its advertising, to such an extent that it had become almost a household word. The British Guianan label is very colourful and as it has long been out of production it is now keenly sought by collectors.

3 *The Arts*

It is a surprise to some people that a homely object like a matchbox should aspire to represent the arts, but actually a wide diversity of cultural subjects has been portrayed. Japan has probably led the field in this type of design; no country has concentrated to such an extent on depicting the various arts for which it is famous. The work of some of the most famous Japanese artists has been shown on labels, the best known being the sets of the reproductions of Ando Hiroshige's drawings of the 53 stations of the Tokaido Road from Tokyo to Kyoto, which he did about 150 years ago. The first of these attractive sets appeared in the late nineteenth century and since then the drawings have been reproduced on a number of sets for boxes of different shapes and sizes. The originals from which the labels were copied were woodcuts and the reproductions have been reduced in size most delicately with little loss of character. There are actually 55 labels in the set, since the two terminal points, as well as the 53 intermediate relay stations, are pictured.

Utamaro's 'ladies' (his famous drawings of courtesans) were the subject for a set of labels for large-size boxes. Beautifully executed in soft colours and first-class printing, the labels were worthy reproductions of a gifted artist's work. In recent years a set of six Japanese labels featured characters from the Bunraku, Japan's classical puppet theatre. These puppets came into being in the seventeenth century with the merging of two different arts—that of the Joruri singer and that of the puppeteer; even today they are one of Japan's most popular entertainments.

Puppets were also the subject of a set of 40 labels on sale in the then Dutch East Indies

1. Full-colour reproduction of Franz Hals' painting 'The Gypsy , from a Mexican set 2. Russian prima ballerina Ulanova, 'king-size' box 3. Spanish insert, late 19th century 4. Printed in England for Swedish matches 5. Japanese label for export to Java, showing Javanese puppets, c1890 6. Modern Chinese label from set of 10 with reproduction of drawing by Chinese artist Chi Pak Shek

many years ago. Printed in Sweden at the turn of the present century, they showed the traditional Javanese puppets and the set is rare today. Japanese labels of the same period, produced for E. M. Nathan of Cheribon and Samarang, also featured the grotesque little figures.

Another modern set of 12 labels from Japan shows the Kabuki theatre, the origin of which is attributed to a female dancer attached to a Shinto shrine who, in 1586, gave performances of somewhat erotic dances. A feature of the Kabuki is that all the parts are traditionally played by men; participation is hereditary and the actors are trained from childhood. The matchbox labels are delightfully drawn and coloured and are a most desirable acquisition for collectors.

Of a different type altogether are the long sets of Mexican all-round labels with excellent reproductions of the Old Masters. One would hesitate before throwing away these boxes when empty. The labels were first issued in the 1950s as the 'Clasicos' set of 'La Central' brand, the fronts showing drawings of the Venus de Milo and the Parthenon in Athens. The reproductions were on the reverse side of the label and included such famous masterpieces as Leonardo da Vinci's 'La Gioconda', Goya's 'La Maja Desnuda' and Franz Hals' 'Gypsy'. All were glazed and the colours were very true to the originals. The labels came in sets of various sizes for boxes which contained varying numbers of wax matches from 34 to 90. In the early 1960s the same firm re-issued the set, but crudely printed on poor-quality card skillets which completely destroyed the beauty of the pictures.

Chopin in the 'Geniuses' set from Mexico

It is to Australia that we must turn for one of the most handsome sets ever produced and representing a unique form of art. In 1965 the Federal Match Co issued for its 'Count 500' size boxes a set of eight labels bearing reproductions of Australian aboriginal bark paintings from Arnhemland, in the far north of the continent.

The labels have a rich gold background and the primitive paintings are reproduced in their original colours. Human figures, often characters from tribal legends, crabs, fish, animals and geometric designs, although simple in concept, are stylishly executed and resemble the prehistoric cave drawings of the early inhabitants of France.

Perhaps more a craft than an art is the lace made so beautifully by the Hungarian peasants, but a set of 12 labels issued in Hungary in 1964 shows clearly the intricate designs created by the lace-makers. Prior to the 1956 uprising in Hungary the peasant women came into Budapest to sell their work, and their traditional site was beneath one of the ochre-coloured walls of the Rosalie Chapel in the centre of the city. There they would squat patiently on the ground, their wares spread before them. It is said that these women would sometimes literally work their fingers to the bone in producing the lace, and specimens bought at their outdoor market occasionally had traces of tiny spots of blood to bear testimony to this. The matchbox labels—obvious 'collectors' labels'—are glossy and the set comprises 1 large box and 11 small boxes, the lace being shown against different coloured backgrounds; the set with a black background is the most effective. The boxes were done up in

1. Reproduction of Utamaro drawing 2. Hara, no. 13 of the 53 stations of the Tokaido Road, Japan

1

2

3

1. Modern Czech set commemorating work of artist Mikolas Ales 2. Popular Austrian brand 3. The 'club'-size label from the Hungarian set of lace designs

1. Alexander Dumas on Mexican skillet in form of his book *The Three Musketeers* 2. Modern set of Polish regional dances 3. Johann Wolfgang Goethe on a Russian label 4. Australian skillet 5. 19th-century Spanish insert, from set of famous pictures in the Spanish National Museum

1

2

3

4

1. One from Czechoslovakian set of 6, 1900 2. Old Austrian label for export to India 3. Japanese, character from Kabuki theatre 4. Modern Czech label from set commemorating 13th Film Festival

souvenir packs and produced mainly as a tourist shopping attraction.

No reference to Russia and the arts would be complete without mention of the ballet and several modern sets of Russian labels have featured celebrated exponents of terpsichore. Prima ballerina Galina Ulanova is the subject of quite a few of them, as on the large-box label of a set of 1 'king' size (as the Russians call it) and 16 small boxes; this is an excellent photogravure reproduction showing her 'on points' in one of her favourite roles. Russia has also recently featured portraits of composers, writers, artists and sculptors on sets of labels, and pictures of Moscow theatres, from the elegant Bolshoi to the building which houses the State Circus. In fact, practically no cultural activity has not been featured on Russian labels during the past five or six years.

The nautch dancers of East India provide a different form of classical entertainment; wearing dresses with full skirts which are attached by loops to their fingers, they look like butterflies as they lift their arms. Two Austrian labels for boxes of matches destined for the Indian market in the early 1900s depicted these dancers, one being entitled 'Nautch Party' and the other 'The Nautch Girl'.

Music has not been featured quite so extensively on labels, but a few years ago a Russian set showed musicians playing their respective instruments in an orchestra with the conductor as the subject of the 'king' size label. There were several sets, each with the same series of designs but each printed in a different colour. The drawings were contemporary in style. Another popular label in this field which comes to mind is an Austrian one printed in black and red on yellow paper and entitled 'Schubert': its central design is a head and shoulders drawing of the composer, partially surrounded by a laurel wreath. A Mexican set of brightly coloured skillets was entitled 'Genios', and among those portrayed was Frederick Chopin, the composer. The title figure of Bizet's opera 'Carmen' was selected as the design for a safety-match label from Finland.

Beautiful women and especially actresses have long been a favourite subject with match manufacturers in several countries. During the latter half of the nineteenth century Spain sold small boxes of tiny wax matches and, in order to prevent these from spilling when the box was opened, a picture card was inserted in the box, rather as cigarette cards were included in packets of cigarettes before world war II. These picture cards were known as 'inserts' and they were issued in sets of each series, the number of the par-

1. Cliff Richard from long Dutch set featuring pop stars 2. The Bolshoi Theatre, modern Russian 'tourist' set of glazed labels 3. From Russian set featuring all instruments in an orchestra 4. Finnish label, c1930s 5. 'King-size' label from Russian 'tourist' set of glazed labels featuring the cinema 6. Crudely-printed Mexican reproduction of an Old Master painting 7. Modern Russian ballet set

ticular design being carefully recorded on the card. The subjects chosen were usually portraits and they ranged from royalty to bullfighters. World-famous actresses of the day featured on at least two sets; an actress selected for portrayal could feel she had really 'made the grade'.

Reproductions of the work of famous artists has appealed to many countries, and in 1962 the distinctive small square matchboxes in China were adorned with a set of 10 labels reproducing the natural-history wash drawings of the late Chi Pak Shek, one of China's most famous artists. Typically oriental in every respect they are printed on thin, almost transparent, paper in black, grey and red.

The younger art of the cinema has found its place on matchbox labels and again Russia has been to the forefront in promoting it. 'The Cinema in the USSR' was a handsome modern set for the tourist trade, the 'king' size label being printed in dignified purple with a clever design of a strip of film in partial shadow, and surmounted by a small motif of two figures raising aloft hammer and sickle in the traditional pose. Several countries have featured films on labels. Czechoslovakia issued a long set of famous scenes—reproductions of actual stills—from award-winning films to commemorate the thirteenth film festival held in that country.

It is perhaps debatable whether 'pop' singing qualifies as an art, but it is included in this chapter and represented by one of a long set of modern Dutch labels which portrayed well-known 'pop' singers from many countries. Cliff Richard, shown on the label illustrated, has actually been pictured in several poses.

4 *Commemorative*

Labels commemorating particular events have always been popular with both manufacturers and collectors. One of their attractions may be that they are usually a limited issue and on sale for only a certain period, so that for the collector they tend to become scarce much more quickly than any other type of design; the Rumanian May Day labels, for example, are on sale for one day only. And as they are often produced to mark important occasions they are usually well-printed and colourful—suited, in fact, to the occasion concerned.

In the early days of matchbox labels royal events were the most popular subject. True to the stiff pomposity of the age, nothing less than a royal occasion was looked upon as worthy of commemoration, although some of the lesser-known manufacturers did branch out to record other things (often local events, such as the opening of a civic building) and it was not long before their lead was generally followed.

Most match-manufacturing countries have produced commemorative labels at some time; nowadays the most enthusiastic producers of commemoratives are the eastern European countries, and here it is often difficult to differentiate between the truly commemorative and the propaganda labels. The early British commemoratives are probably the most sought-after labels in the world today and, when put up for sale, they usually command the highest prices.

The majority of these early British labels were of the all-round-the-box type: that is, the label wrapped completely around the outer cover of the box and was printed on front and back panels, as well as on one side, the other side being filled by the striking abrasive. Such labels are, of course, still in use today, but in the early days the boxes were much larger and the matches correspondingly clumsy, with thick stems and large heads.

'The Imperial Topical Match' label is an example of the type and size of label common in those days. This one is actually a great rarity, the

1 2 3 4 5

1. Royal visit to Canada 1959 2. 8th Czechoslovak Film Festival 1954 3. Coronation of King George VI and Queen Elizabeth in England 1937. Cingalese label 4. From a set of 6 labels to commemorate ten years of the 'liberation' of Hungary, 1955 5. Queen Wilhelmina's Fund for Dutch flood victims 1953

illustration showing the only one *known* to exist, although there may well be other, unrecorded copies. Issued in the year 1887 to commemorate the Manchester Exhibition, it was a purely 'local' issue, on sale in the north only. Queen Victoria was a popular subject for British commemoratives, her long reign being conducive to the production of quite a number. The single top label for the 'Diamond Jubilee Match' came in a great many variations of printing, paper and wording, and Sweden did, in fact, feature the Queen on several different issues.

Nowadays royal occasions are not commemorated so frequently but there have still been some nice modern issues on the theme. On the occasion of the visit to Canada in 1950 of Queen Elizabeth II and the Duke of Edinburgh, the Eddy Match Company issued an attractive skillet bearing on both panels a charming photograph of the royal couple, reproduced in natural colours. This was a very limited issue, many collectors never succeeding in securing a sample.

Not quite so flamboyant was another British all-round-the-box label, issued by Messrs Moreland & Son Ltd, the Gloucester match manufacturers, to commemorate the visit of the Queen and the Duke to their city on 3 May 1955. The label was printed on white art paper, with a reproduction of the city arms printed in red, dark blue and gold on the front, and on the back a few appropriate words of welcome from the City of Gloucester. The boxes were actually produced for a banquet held by the civic authorities in honour of the royal couple, one box being placed by each table setting. After the initial, very limited, printing the blocks were destroyed, so

1. Royal visit to Gloucester, England 1955 2. Universal & International Exhibition, Belgium 1958 3. Swedish 'customers'' label to commemorate Wembley Exhibition, England 1924 4. Russian label in honour of space dog 'Daring' 1959 5. 11th Sokol Festival, Prague 1948. Czechoslovakian label 6. Congress of Spice Importers, Hälsingborg, Sweden 1956 7. Italian all-round-the-box label commemorating Holy Year 1950, from a set of 9 8. Swedish label issued to commemorate Queen Victoria's Diamond Jubilee

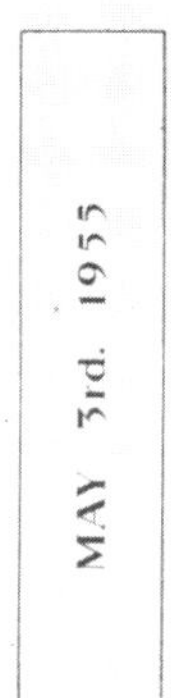

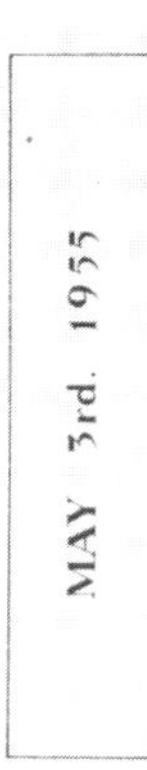

1

2

3

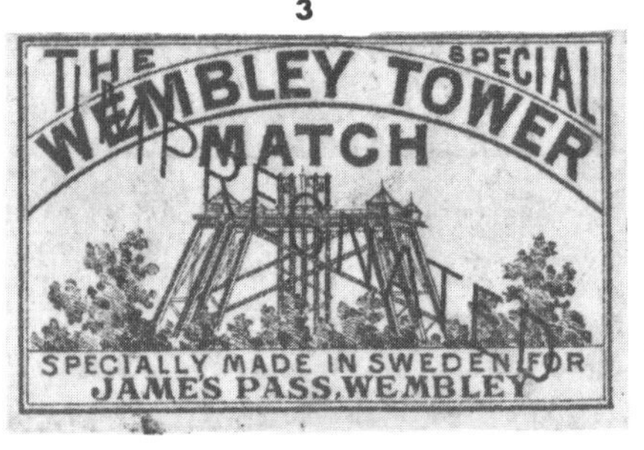

4

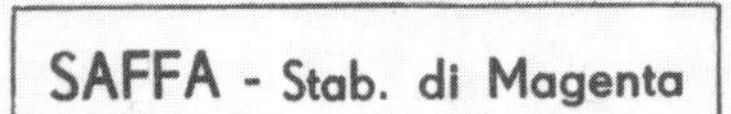

7

5

6

8

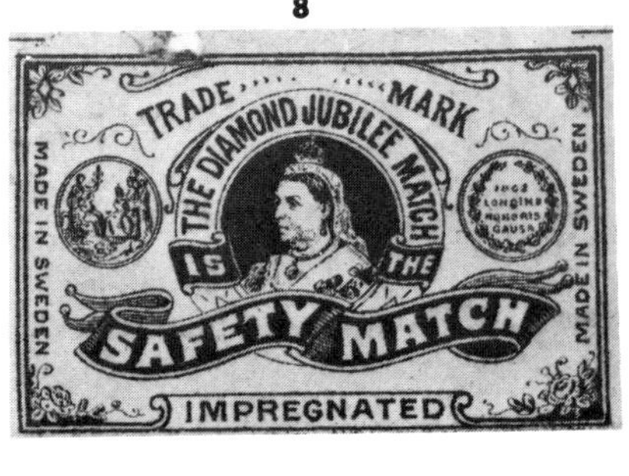

that there will be no reprints in the future.

Just such a reprint spoilt the rarity potential of another all-round label issued to commemorate a royal occasion. This was the one put on the market at the time of the coronation of King George VI and Queen Elizabeth in 1937, and produced by the now-defunct North of England Match Co Ltd. Entitled 'Commonwealth Matches', the red, white and blue label showed the Union flag and was eagerly sought by collectors. But a later reprint spoilt its future as a rare item and now copies repose in a great many collections.

Very different were the two all-round labels used to demonstrate the first automatic match-labelling machines at the world exhibition in Paris in 1900. The labels were printed on machines shown working and the boxes were given away to spectators as souvenirs. The front of the labels commemorated the exhibition, the reverse had the advertisement of Gerhard Arehn, the manufacturer of match-making machines. One is illustrated.

Exhibitions were and of course still are a favourite subject for commemorative labels. The Wembley Exhibition of 1924-5 was, rather surprisingly, not popular for many label designs, but one enterprising firm cashed in on it to promote its own name: James Pass of Wembley had 'The Special Wembley Tower Match' made in Sweden and the design showed one of the landmarks of the Exhibition grounds.

The Universal & International Exhibition in Brussels in 1958 brought forth a spate of labels but unfortunately many of them, produced in Belgium, were merely 'collectors' labels' and never intended to adorn matchboxes. Of those which did go into use on boxes, the majority incorporated one or other of the symbols created to represent and publicise the exhibition. The designs were all very modern and symbolic and a complete contrast to the Wembley ones of earlier years, a significant comment on how tastes have changed over the years.

1. Rare old Swedish label commemorating first of the automatic match-labelling machines exhibited, Paris 1900 2. 70th birthday of Generalissimo Chiang Kai Shek

Not an exhibition but a festival stimulated a label from the USA. Each year in New England when the apple blossom is at its best an Apple Festival is held, people crowding into the region to see the lovely orchards and the various events such as carnival processions based on the theme of apple blossom. This usually starts each year on 1 May and a safety-match label was issued a few years ago to mark the occasion, printed appropriately in red and green on white paper.

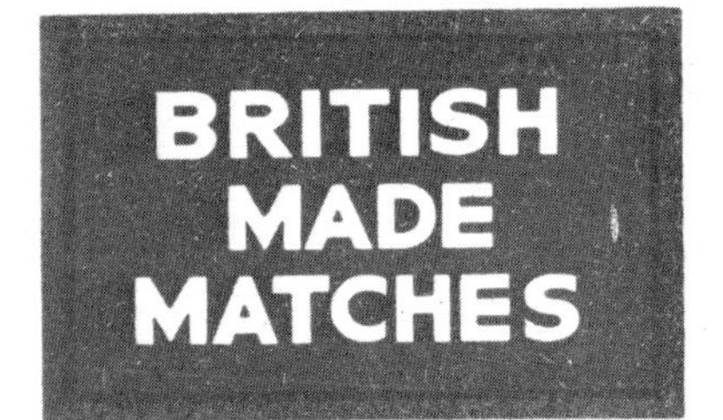

2

3

4

5

6

HEROICAL

CHELIUSKIN

MADE IN USSR SAFETY MATCHES AVERAGE 50 MATCHES

Made by
NORTH OF ENGLAND MATCH CO. LTD.
WEST HARTLEPOOL, COUNTY DURHAM.

1

7

8

1. Coronation commemorative, 1937 2. An American occasion 3. American flood disaster 1936 4. 750th anniversary of the city of Dresden 1956. East German label 5. First label in the Australian set of 64 issued for Olympic Games, Melbourne 1956 6. Russian Polar Expedition rescued; issued for export, 1935 7. 200th anniversary of Swedish newspaper *Berlingske Tidende* 8. Early British label commemorating Capt Webb's Channel swim, 1875

This was again a label sponsored by a commercial undertaking as part of its own publicity campaign.

Feats of valour not unnaturally invite commemoration, and the match manufacturers have always risen to the occasion, giving the collector many worthwhile items. In 1934 Professor Schmidtz's Polar Expedition ran into trouble, 101 men and women being trapped when their ship SS *Chelyushkin* was crushed by pack ice whilst attempting the North-East Passage. They were able to set up a makeshift camp on the ice and after enduring great hardship were finally rescued by seven pilots of the Soviet Air Force, who showed outstanding bravery by landing planes in most dangerous conditions and were all later awarded the decoration of Hero of the Soviet Union.

The incident aroused much public admiration and in 1935 the Russian match industry issued two labels commemorating it. One was designed for export, and was entitled 'Heroical Safety Match'; with English wording it shows the areoplanes coming in to land for the rescue. The other label was for home sale, and was issued a few months later; it showed the same scene, but with slight variations in the drawing. A little later another export label on the theme was issued. This was entitled 'Help Safety Matches' and showed the ship trapped in the ice, with an aeroplane flying towards it. Although printed in quantity at the time these labels are quite scarce today.

Among the diverse subjects chosen for commemoration, the record for the most extraordinary design must surely go to the Japanese for their black and yellow label entitled 'The Ceylon Sensation Rock Safety Matches' commemorating the accession to the Belgian throne of King Leopold II! When the first railway engine was put into use in Ceylon in 1864 the Duke of Brabant travelled by special train to Ambepussa to open the line, although it was not actually completed until 1867; part of the route was a steep zig-zag ascent up a mountain and along the edge of a dangerous precipice known as Sensation Rock. So when the Duke of Brabant later came to the Belgian throne, this label was issued showing a train travelling along the narrow stretch of track.

Very rare British label commemorating Manchester Exhibition 1887

The stories commemorated by labels are not always happy. The late Queen (afterwards Princess) Wilhelmina of the Netherlands sponsored several which, strictly, fell into what is

1. Modern Italian skillet commemorating centenary of Battle of Magenta 1859. Italian Centenary series 1959 2. Japanese label commemorating accession of King Leopold II of Belgium 3. Olympic Games, Stockholm, 1956. Swedish 4. World Co-op Week 1965. Iranian 5. Independence of Nigeria 1960. Nigerian

known as the 'charity label' category but which also served to mark important events in her country's history. After the disastrous floods in February 1953 which devastated much of the country, the label for the KWF (Koningin Wilhelmina Fund) bore a simple design of a badly-damaged home partly submerged by flood waters; the matches were sold at 3 cents a box, all proceeds being devoted to the fund, which had been started by the Queen to aid the flood victims. The date—1 Feb 1953—on the label turned it also into an interesting commemorative item.

Another flood disaster was recorded when, in the 1930s, the city of Johnstown, Pennsylvania, USA, was badly damaged. A matchbox label was one of the means employed in campaigning for more and better dams in the areas where floods were regularly experienced.

A commemorative label which attained scarcity value was issued for the eighth Czechoslovakian Film Festival, held at Karlovy Vary (formerly Karlsbad) in 1954. Only 2,000 copies of this attractive label were printed and it appears that almost all these finally came to rest in collections, mainly of course in Czechoslovakia, where enthusiasts are many. The design is a photograph of the famous stag statue in Karlovy, erected on the spot where legend tells that one of King Charles IV's hounds, out hunting with its master, chanced upon the first of the thermal springs which later brought prosperity to the area. The top half of the label is covered with a drawing of a piece of film, and wording is kept to the minimum.

Achievements in space have inspired Russian designers to produce a series of labels starting with Sputnik 1 and continuing with portraits of the first men, woman and dogs in space. The very first of these now commonplace designs is illustrated. It traces the satellite's circumference of the world and beneath the date, 1957, the inscription reads 'Our satellites embrace the Earth'. The much-fêted Yuri Gagarin was the first spaceman to appear on a label and after space-dog Laika other dogs were featured; the illustration shows one which returned safely, the popular Daring, with the inscription 'Dog "Daring" 10 July 1959 in 4 (seconds?) once raised into the cosmos'.

Sport has come in for its fair share of commemoration on matchbox labels (with the Olympic Games one of the most popular subjects) although, strangely, some years have produced a far greater crop of sporting labels than others. The XIVth Olympiad in 1956 was of course an inspiration, with labels appearing in many countries, notably of course in Australia, where the Games were held in Melbourne. There a set of 64 labels printed in red and blue on white paper depicted all the sports included in the Games.

Australia was the country of origin of another sporting label which caused some controversy when it appeared. Printed in blue and black on semi-art paper, it bore an off-shore photograph of the yacht *Gretel*, Australia's challenger in the Americas Cup race in 1962, and was issued by the Federal Match Co. But because it was used only as a reverse label on boxes which carried a different Federal label on the front, many collectors considered it only a 'collectors'' item and not a genuine label. So strong were the arguments that a statement was issued confirming that it was a genuine label.

One of the great feats recorded was the swimming of the English Channel on 24 August 1875 by Captain Webb. Britain's Diamond Match Co was quick to come out with an all-round-the-box label showing on the front a portrait of the captain and on the reverse a picture of him actually performing his feat of endurance. Variations of this label appeared for many years and when the

1

2

3

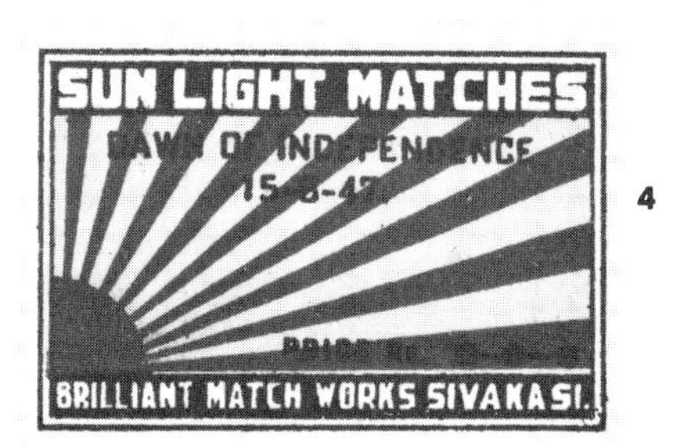

4

1. Packet label from Belgian set commemorating a tragedy of world war II 2. Russian label commemorating the Sputnik I, 1957 3. Formation of Malaysia 1954 4. Independence of India 1947

1

2

3

4

1. America's Cup Yacht Race 1962. Australian label 2. Yuri Gagarin, first man in space, 1961. Russian label 3. From set of 3 labels commemorating heroic Yugoslavian partisan stand in the mountains during world war II 4. From set of 5 Yugoslavian labels commemorating 20th anniversary of Yugoslav entry into world war II

Diamond Match Co was taken over by Bryant & May Ltd the design was still retained. Over the years it was gradually modernised, the most noticeable difference in one recent version being that the Captain's swimming costume has been made tolerable to modern eyes by being shown as much briefer than that of the earlier versions! In 1961 the design was changed to a head and shoulders portrait only.

Mention must also be made of another short series of modern labels with a story behind them, the Czechoslovakian 1948 Sokol labels. For 86 years the pride of Czechoslovakia had been the great Sokol festival, a sort of combined Olympiad and patriotic rally, at which the Czechs showed themselves as undisputed experts in mass calisthenics. During the Nazi occupation of the country desperate efforts were made to destroy the Sokol, both spiritually and physically, but all efforts in that direction failed. The 1948 festival was notable for being the first held under the new régime, and attempts were made to turn the Sokol into something more approaching a political propaganda rally. But this also failed and the eleventh Sokol, so widely publicised on matchbox labels, remained the patriotic athletic event that it had always been. Even the labels were printed in red, white and blue and not the all-red with black lettering which the organisers had desired.

5 *Costume*

Costume is a colourful, attractive and popular subject, and many countries have issued matchbox labels depicting not only their own national dress but that of other lands. The accuracy of the costume pictures is often remarkable and the colours are usually selected with care and an eye to detail. Quite a number of collectors specialise in these labels, and their albums are usually a joy to behold.

In some countries native costume is still worn every day, but in others, particularly in Europe, it is only brought out for special occasions such as festivals or celebrations. Climatic conditions and the local materials available have in most cases been the deciding factor in the design of any particular costume, although various other circumstances have brought modifications over the years.

1. One of the rare Polish set labels of the early 1930s, showing man and children in costume of Gorale region 2. From modern Japanese set of 10 national costumes 3. Old Japanese label 4. Label from one of Spanish sets of 35 showing regional costumes of Spain 5. Man of Brittany; label from modern French set 6. Israeli costume on label from set issued in Belgium 1938 to commemorate Universal & International Exhibition. Label reads 'Welcome to Belgium' 7. From set of 12 Czechoslovakian labels showing costumes of the country 8. Latvian label 9. Modern set of Polish dances and costumes 10. Modern French label, one of set of 6 showing costumes of French provinces 11. One of the most popular Swedish sets of costume labels. Woman of Dalarna from the 'purple background' set of 12, issued 1935 12. Early Swedish label, one of a highly-glazed pair

The central European countries are a rich source of costume labels. Poland has issued some delightful ones, including a series of sets which are now rare. Put on sale in the 1930s, these sets (each of 6 different labels) portrayed in full colour the costumes worn by men, women and children in different regions of the country. The sheepskin coat, lavishly decorated with braid and coloured cut-leather shapes, is considered by experts to show the original influence of Asiatic horsemen who entered Europe via Russia. The label from one of the rare sets which is illustrated shows a man from the Görale region wearing just such a coat, although these people are farmers rather than horsemen or horse breeders, and he is shown with rake and scythe over his shoulder. Another Polish label which is illustrated (also one of a set) shows a man and woman folk-dancing, and although not visible in the label picture the girl will be wearing several of the necklaces of amber, coral and glass which are distinctive to the region.

1 & 2. Hungarian costume sets of the 1950s, showing shepherd of the Great Hungarian Plain and woman of the Boldog region 3. Early 20th-century Swedish label showing woman in costume of Södermanland 4. Swedish label for export to Greece with woman in Greek costume

Hungary is another country where much pride is shown in the native costumes, although again they are now only worn on special occasions and for folk-dancing performances. The Hungarian women's costume includes a full skirt, ankle or knee length (often magnificently embroidered), worn over several petticoats, and a blouse with puffed sleeves. A heavily embroidered apron often completes the picture. A few years ago Hungary issued eight sets of labels, each containing 6 designs, showing men's and women's costume for different parts of the country. The sets were printed in two colours only on various pale shades of paper but in each set the same 9 costumes were shown. The man from Hortobägy, the great plain of Hungary, wears the region's fine sleeved coat—the original source of the Magyar sleeve beloved of modern fashion—decorated with coloured bands and motifs, together with the hard felt hat used for protection against the weather. This outfit again may have been influenced by the clothes of the Mongol horsemen of the steppes who used the old caravan routes and invaded many countries during their travels.

Czechoslovakia is another rich source of costume labels. Here too the emphasis is on embroidery, especially in Moravia, but the label illustrated (one of a set of 12) shows a more simple female working dress, whilst the man wears a sheepskin coat; both men and women wear thick puttees wound around their legs.

In the country districts of Greece the finest national dress comes out for weddings: a miniature-size box label for matches made in Sweden and intended for export to Greece showed a woman in all her finery, her costume richly embroidered with gold, and adorned with coin necklaces and a string of coins suspended from the waist in the form of a short apron.

France has a great variety of regional costumes, the majority of them now worn only on gala occasions. A few years ago a series of attractively-designed labels was issued showing the costumes of France and also those of French

1. Modern US skillet, one of set of 6 2. Finland, pre-1939 3. Italian export label 4. Egyptian label for the home market, the woman wearing the modern 'see-through' yashmak 5. Peruvian Indian on Austrian label for export to Peru 6. Label from Macao

possessions overseas. The drawings are simple but graphically done against brightly-coloured backgrounds and the sets each contain 6 labels. They proved very popular with collectors and came in several variations as each factory printed its own identification mark in the bottom corners.

Sweden has exploited to the full its wide variety of regional costumes and all the labels are typically well-produced. A particularly attractive set of 12 issued in 1935 has remained popular with collectors ever since, and was later reprinted. It shows the peasant dress of both men and women, the drawings standing out against an impressive purple background. One label from the set is illustrated, showing a woman of Orsa in Dalarne. In Sweden one of the special occasions when such costumes come out is Midsummer Eve, a great Scandinavian festival. A feature of all of them is their weaving and much of the material used is home-dyed with vegetable dyes; embroidery is also much to the fore. The small label illustrated of a woman in costume from Södermanland shows the becoming stiffened-linen cap.

In 1935 Spain issued what have become two classic sets of 35 labels each, showing men and women in the dress of various regions of Spain. With glossy finish, these were tinted reproductions of photographs, so all detail is accurate. Both sets are keenly sought by collectors. Many of the Spanish costumes are simple, but the women's shawls are usually very beautiful. The men's dress tends to be sombre.

A relatively scarce set of labels issued in the early 1930s by the Swedish Match Co depicted men's and women's costumes of the various Dutch provinces, but although the drawings are good the labels are somewhat disappointing in that the printing is in black and red only, on yellow paper, which does not do full justice to

1. Swedish label, one of set showing costumes of Holland 2. Early 20th-century Swedish export label 3. One of set of Finnish labels, early 1930s, showing women in regional dress of Mouhijärvi and Porvoon Pitäjä

the subject.

The costume of other nations further afield has also been depicted on labels, although not always by home manufacturers. For instance 'The Abyssinian' issued in Sweden in the 1920s had a most carefully-executed drawing of an Abyssinian woman wearing the long flowing robe and the magnificent necklace and bracelets which are characteristic of the country.

Japanese national dress is world famous: the women's graceful kimono held in position by the wide obi or waistband is recognised everywhere. Japanese matchbox labels have naturally portrayed this on many occasions, but an unusual set of 10 issued in the early 1960s shows costumes from other countries—including Scotland!

The illustration of the costumes of other peoples of the world is, indeed, becoming popular among match manufacturers. A set issued in Belgium at the time of the International Exhibition in 1958 depicted men and women in costume from many different countries; a novel touch was the printing of the words 'Welcome to Belgium' on each label in the language and script of the country whose costume was shown. This attractive set was issued by a well-known Belgian cigarette firm, and shows that an advertising label (not usually very popular) can please collectors. The label from this set which is illustrated shows a woman from Israel wearing the costume which is, alas, now almost extinct in that country.

A Burmese woman features on a multi-coloured label from Burma, showing the long straight skirt (usually made in soft Burmese silk, but sometimes in cotton when worn by the less well-to-do) and the loose cotton jacket; flowers are often entwined in a tightly drawn-up hair style. In Arab countries the portrayal of veiled women for any purpose is frowned upon, but a small Egyptian label broke the bonds of convention by using a drawing of an up-to-date Arab woman wearing the modern 'see-through' yashmak.

By contrast, Finland portrayed an Eskimo on a matchbox label. Traditional Eskimo clothing for both sexes consists of trousers made of sealskin as well as sealskin boots, fur side out, and bead decoration is sometimes found on the best dress of the women. On the label, however, the clothes can hardly be described as traditional because the man appears to be wearing a thick wool sweater.

The American Indians need no introduction, especially the chiefs with their feathered head-dresses and buckskin leggings. One of the best portrayals comes, naturally, on an American skillet, one of a set of six issued by the Diamond Match Co of New York in recent years for its Diamond 'Domino' matches, illustrating aspects of outdoor life in the USA. Beautifully-executed drawings are reproduced in brown ink on white card, the front of the box in question having a detailed drawing of the head of an Indian in the full finery of his feathered head-dress, and the reverse side showing a squaw with a papoose on her back, paddling a typical Indian dug-out canoe.

Costume labels can be classed as the most innocuous of them all: it cannot be recalled that any have ever caused offence or that any complaint about them has ever come from any source—something which cannot be said for all matchbox label designs.

6 *Flowers and Fruit*

For decoration anywhere, at any time, people turn first to flowers; match manufacturers and matchbox label designers have of course employed them, along with their fruits, to decorate labels throughout the world. The most illustrated flower? Probably the rose, which pops up in a variety of shapes and sizes from a great many countries. And the roses shown are, with very few exceptions, fullblown and frequently coloured red or pink.

But high in popularity with those who select label designs is a more unusual flower, the edelweiss (*gnaphalium leontopodium* to give its full title), that small, white, woolly plant and flower of the aster family which is native to the Alps. Its reputation for growing in inaccessible spots has probably arisen from its liking for high, rocky places which are difficult of access anyway, and not from any innate tendency to play hard to get! Nevertheless, this reputation provides a lucrative income for some people in popular mountain resorts, as they gather and dry or press edelweiss and sell it in small bunches, at often exorbitant prices, to enthusiastic tourists. The fact that the plant is now appearing in many seedsmen's catalogues for growing in one's own rock garden will probably knock the bottom out of that market! Countries which have featured it on matchbox labels include, naturally, Austria, as well as the USA, where a firm in Chicago distributed matches showing a bunch of

1

2

3

4

5

1. Edelweiss from Austria 2. Scabious from modern Dutch set 3. The flame grevillia from the set of 64 labels showing the flora of Australia 4. Pineapples, from a set of 64 labels depicting the industries of Australia 5. Alpine flowers on a Swiss label

1. Japanese label of the 1920s 2. Swedish label in honour of famous botanist Linnaeus 3. Egyptian rose 4. A popular Belgian export label of the 1940s 5. Betel nut and leaf on Japanese label for export to East Africa 6. Chilli peppers from India.

dainty edelweiss.

Alpines have appeared on labels from several mountainous countries; as with animals and birds, countries tend to depict on their labels the flowers and fruit which are indigenous to them. This gives them a double popularity—with the local population to whom they are familiar and therefore appeal as likely to be a trustworthy product, and with collectors to whom they are a novelty. The Swiss Alpine plant labels are among the prettiest issued, and the edelweiss, gentian and pink Alpine rose invariably appear. To some older people the gentian has a further attraction, quite apart from the beauty of its brilliant blue trumpet-like flowers: certain varieties of this bitter herb have tonic roots which they revere as medicine.

A Japanese label for export to India was entitled 'Tambu Popo' and showed a leaf and fruit of the betel nut, a climbing type of pepper which grows in the East Indies. The leaves, wrapped round a few slices of the nutlike seed and a little shell lime, are chewed by the natives, much as in more advanced countries people chew gum. The red juice is periodically spat out by the chewer, which can hardly be described as an

1. Edelweiss from USA 2. Czechoslovakian export label 3. Stylised azaleas from USA

endearing habit. More palatable to Western taste is another type of pepper shown on several labels from India, the chilli, the dried ripe pod of the red pepper which is enjoyed by those who like 'hot' food.

The lychee or Chinese strawberry appropriately adorns a matchbox from China and 'Tjap Duren' ('Duren Matches') from Indonesia shows the globular pulpy fruit of the tree *durio zibethinus*, which is cultivated in the Malay Archipelago. Japan offers 'Fuji Cherry' Brand with a spray of cherry blossom in front of an outline drawing of Mount Fuji. 'The Grape' from Belgium will remind tourists that during the summer in that country hundreds of little stalls by the roadside invite motorists to stop and purchase delectable bunches.

One of the most handsome of all flower labels was also one of the cleverest with a twist in the title. The long-defunct firm of Taylor & Co of Mitcham Lane, Merton, London, put its 'Merton Monster' brand on the market in the nineteenth century. An all-round-the-box label printed in red on white paper described the contents of the box as 'The Pink of Perfection'—the design being a large full-blown pink (*dianthus*) and two buds. Copies now repose in most of the 'top collections', to be envied by those still seeking what has become a very elusive item.

Flowers are of course ideal subjects for long sets of labels. Japan has featured them on several occasions and one modern set of 50 labels has included several less well-known varieties of flora such as the horsetail, that rather curious plant of the cryptogamous genus *equisetum*, which when fully open has whorls of branches like the hairs in a horse's tail—only the Japanese design, just to be different, shows the 'tail' in bud form. A modern Australian set of 64 depicts in full colour a wide range of the wild flowers of Australia, all beautiful and including many not found elsewhere.

The modern British 'Variety' sets made by Bryant & May feature clear drawings in natural colour, plus a short description, of several British wild plants; another modern set of labels on the

The famous and rare old British 'Merton Monster'

1

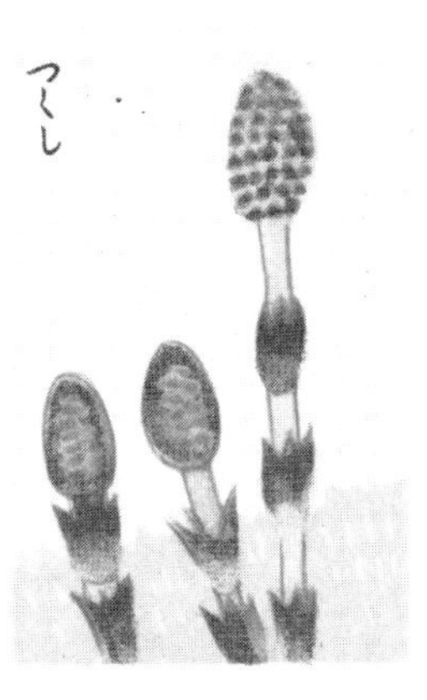

2

3

4

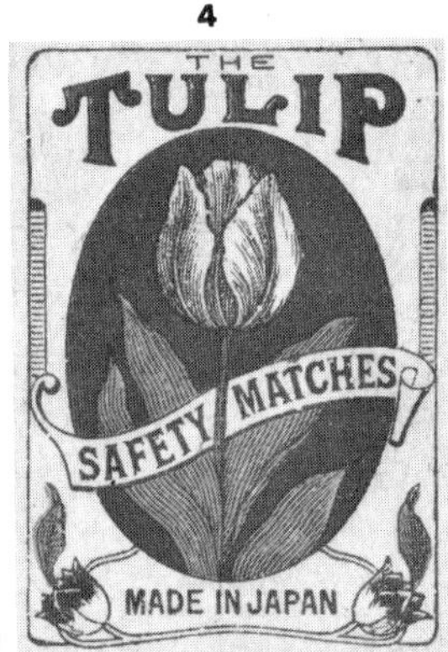

5

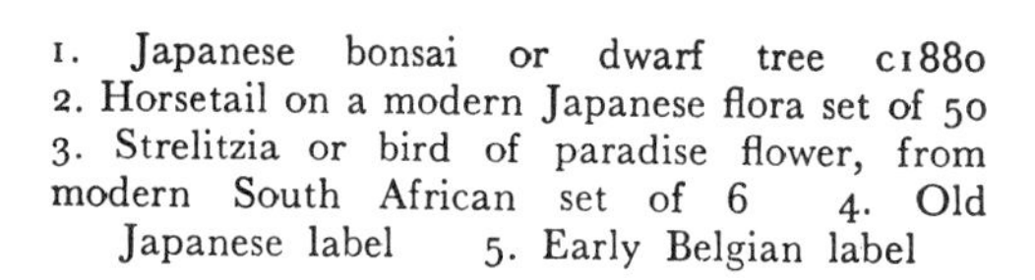
1. Japanese bonsai or dwarf tree c1880 2. Horsetail on a modern Japanese flora set of 50 3. Strelitzia or bird of paradise flower, from modern South African set of 6 4. Old Japanese label 5. Early Belgian label

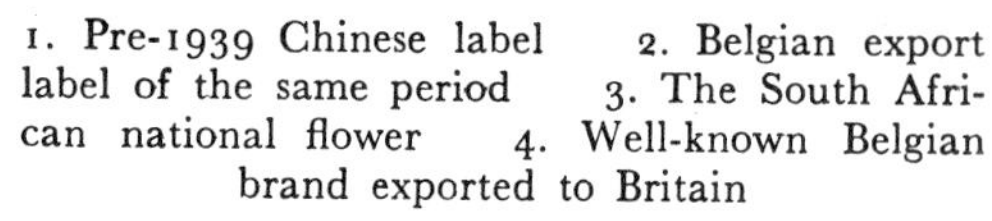
1. Pre-1939 Chinese label 2. Belgian export label of the same period 3. The South African national flower 4. Well-known Belgian brand exported to Britain

1

2

3

4

1. The Ghent, Belgium, Flower Show label, 1955 2. Product of the Benelux countries for export to Africa 3. Belgian export label, similar to one from Czechoslovakia 4. Austrian set put on sale in England, c1959 5. The controversial Czechoslovakian 'Flanders Poppy' label 6. Lotus—the national flower of Egypt on an Egyptian label 7. One of a modern set of 6 from South Africa

British market comes from the Solo works of Austria and shows colour photographs of popular flowers. A somewhat similar set from South Africa includes the exotic *strelitzia* or Bird of Paradise flower.

National emblems also feature as matchbox label designs, for instance the protea from South Africa and the lotus from Egypt, the latter shown in the conventional archaeological representation. This Egyptian water-lily, incidentally is not considered to be the plant which gives its name to the fruit mentioned in Homer's *Odyssey* which was said to induce a dreamy languor in those who ate it.

Flowers one would think to be 'safe' subjects for matchbox labels, offering no opportunities for controversy. Yet in fact they have on occasion caused as much trouble as a political or religious design could do. A mild storm arose in Belgian horticultural circles when an orchid was chosen to decorate the label advertising the 1955 Ghent flower show, because some people did not consider it was the turn of the orchid growers to provide a design. And the British Legion complained when a Czechoslovakian label on boxes of matches on sale in Britain a few years ago showed a poppy resembling the Legion's Flanders poppy emblem. Flower and fruit labels offer their crop of spelling mistakes too, especially if they come from India or Japan—both countries notoriously bad spellers of English words on labels. 'Pomagranat' is the phonetic title of an Indian label; this label does not, as one would expect, depict that well-known fruit of a North African and West Asiatic tree which children often love but which adults class as having too thick and tough a rind, too many seeds and too acid a red pulp; it shows a spray of the unfamiliar and attractive red bell-like flowers from which the fruit develops.

New Zealand is one of the few countries in the world which still produce small cylindrical boxes of wax matches. 'Fern Brand' has long been a famous New Zealand mark on ordinary matchbox labels, but the distinctive tiny round label entitled 'Fern Brand', with appropriately enough the design of a fern, which is stuck on the end lid of the cylindrical boxes is in some demand. Very few of these 'pillbox' labels are issued, though sixty years ago quite a selection was available.

An unusual horticultural label from Japan, untitled, shows something typical of that country—a bonsai or miniature tree. The cultivation of these is a traditional interest in Japan and is fast becoming popular in America and in Britain. Some of the trees are several hundred years old and valued at sums running into four figures. Flowering varieties are particularly desirable—and the one on the Japanese label is in full flower. Another unexpected subject is seen on a Swedish label entitled 'Linnea'; this pays tribute

1

2

3

4

5

6

7

8

1. British skillet of 6, issued 1960s 2. Mangoes from India 3. Pre-world war II Finnish label 4. Pillbox label from New Zealand 5. Fruit of the tree *durio zibethinus* from Indonesia 6. Belgian label of the late 1920s 7. Pomegranate flowers from India 8. The cherry blossom of Japan

to the celebrated Swedish botanist Linnaeus (Carolus Karl von Linne) who, during his lifetime from 1707 to 1778, founded a System of Botany which gave a great impulse to the more scientific study of plants.

7 *Geography*

UNDER THIS broad heading can be included the myriads of labels which depict famous places, buildings and scenery, for there can be hardly a tourist attraction in the world from the Mexican Pyramid of the Sun to Beachy Head which has not been shown. In addition to the famous sights of the world, countless more obscure ones have been the subject of label titles and designs, usually for purely local issues, circulating only in areas where a brand bearing the name of a nearby building or beauty spot could be assured of a good sale.

It is these purely local issues which particularly attract the label collector, and which are becoming increasingly scarce. In the age of the motor car and the aeroplane fewer and fewer places are remaining off the beaten track, and if a sight is worth seeing, whether it be scenery or a church, it soon becomes nationally, even world, famous. The result is that fewer and fewer local labels are being produced. Another reason for this is the disappearance of the small manufacturers, particularly in Britain, who were usually the producers of limited-appeal labels.

1

2

3

4

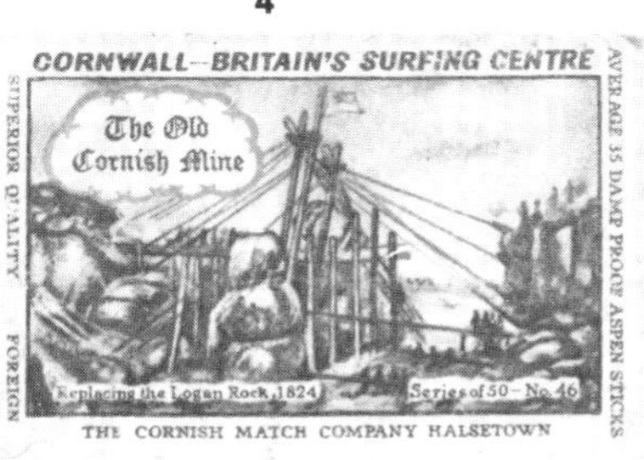

5

1. From a set of 10 softly-coloured labels for Russian matches distributed in Britain 2. The famous Taj Mahal on an Indian label 3. Rare old Austrian label for export to Turkey 4. Replacing the Logan Rock, Cornwall, toppled by vandals in 1824. One of a set of 50 labels for Russian matches distributed in the south-west of England in 1966 5. The Fisherman's Bastion, Budapest. One of a set of views of Budapest issued in Hungary, mid-1960s.

1. Label for 'drawing-room' matches from Switzerland showing map of the country and principal industries 2. Old Swedish export label for UK 3. Rare old Austrian label 4. Early Russian label for export to UK 5. Map of Denmark on a Danish label for the home market 6. Recent Austrian label printed for government of Andorra 7. Belgian label for export to Britain in the early 1960s

A specialised collection of geographical labels could be begun by gathering together those depicting maps; the accumulation would not be large, but would be very fascinating. In Switzerland a great trade with tourists is done in large-size 'household' or 'drawing-room' boxes of matches adorned with handsome glossy labels depicting various aspects and attractions of the country. One of these labels is a map of Switzerland, roughly showing the main contours of the country and the rail links into it from all parts of Europe, whilst little illustrations pin point areas famous for certain things—a St. Bernard dog stands by the St Bernard Pass, a figure of William Tell near Lac Leman, etc. There is no wording on the label but it is identified as Swiss by the two trade-marks which appear on all modern Swiss labels: in the bottom left-hand corner a tiny device of five balls around a central stem with another crossing it and the word 'label' written beneath; in the right-hand corner a minute cross-bow device and the initials 'EZ' (Etincelle Zundholtzer, the factory of manufacture).

The United Kingdom has been featured on labels from Sweden and from Russia, to name but two. The Swedish issue (dating from the early twentieth century) had a red outline map with Edinburgh, London and Dublin marked. This brought protests from some Welshmen, who thought it unfair that Wales's largest city was missing, but research into the history of the label indicates that it was never used on boxes sold in Wales. Other 'map' labels include those showing Australia—a rather rare old Australian label entitled 'Commonwealth Safety Matches'—Denmark, Cyprus, the tiny Andorra, India, North America, the Isle of Wight, and the English counties of Cornwall and Dorset.

Many match producers have of course depicted outstanding features of their own countries. A skillet (actually a 'spring-flap' box of the type much favoured in the Latin countries) from Argentina shows a map of South America with Argentina coloured in on the front, and on the reverse a natural-colour representation of the enormous statue which is one of the country's prides—Christ of the Andes. This statue, at an altitude of 13,500 ft on the Andean Divide, was erected jointly by the Argentinian and Chilean governments in 1902 as a symbol of international accord; it has been likened to the Statue of Liberty, but the only thing the two have in common is their size.

One of Britain's modern wonders was the Clifton Suspension Bridge at Bristol, that elegant structure across the Avon Gorge which marked such a tremendous achievement in bridge building. A Dutch label for 'The Clifton Suspension Bridge Impregnated' paid tribute to it and a Belgian label of similar design was also issued.

1

2

1. Christ of the Andes—Argentinian skillet 2. Old American label showing an artist's impression of one of the Egyptian sphinxes

Landscapes, like flowers, freely lend themselves to pictorial representation, and match manufacturers have eagerly grasped the opportunity of making their boxes attractive and also interesting to the purchaser. The first landscape labels showed scenery for its own value as a pretty picture, but with the growth of tourism throughout the world more and more countries use

1

2

3

4

5

6

7

8

1. Famous Greek landmark on a Yugoslavian label for export to Greece 2. Beautifully-coloured, glazed label for 'club'-size box. One of set of 15 showing historic German cities, produced in West Germany, 1950-60 3. Italian skillet with woodcut scenes of Venice, c1949 4. One of modern Austrian set of 12 views of London 5. Rumanian label showing Scântia Publishing House, Bucharest, c1955 6. View of Kashmir on an Indian label for export to Burma 7. Seaside resort of Marsa, Tunisia, Czechoslovakian, c1962 8. The Wailing Wall, Jerusalem, one of short set of labels from Palestine issued before the ending of the British mandate and showing features of the country

matchboxes for inviting advertising of the charms of their respective areas; the result is better and better printing and more attention to selecting the best possible viewpoint. Tunisia was early in on this idea (just one of the ways in which it proved itself an up-and-coming country), issuing a series of labels depicting in full colour its fast-developing seaside resorts—Monastir, Hammamet, Sousse, Marsa, etc. The labels are printed in Czechoslovakia to adorn boxes of Czechoslovakian matches and they are available in hotels, tourist offices and similar establishments in Tunisia.

Germany used perfectly-produced reproductions from colour photographs of some of its beautiful old towns for a set of 15 labels for large boxes, and these proved a best-selling line to tourists and local inhabitants alike. The one illustrated shows Würzburg, with its fine old bridge and Marienburg fortress on the hill.

Matchbox labels can also give glimpses of rarely-seen features of a place. An Indian label of a few years ago issued for a firm in Rangoon was entitled ' Dal Lake Kashmir ' and illustrated a native boat of the region being poled across the lake by a woman wearing the local dress. It could almost be a scene on the River Thames, except that mountains are visible in the background, and is a homely glimpse of a part of the world which is often over-glamourised. A short Israeli set of labels depicted views of Jerusalem, including, strangely, the famous Wailing Wall, the last remaining part of Solomon's Temple. When the set was issued the Wall was actually in the Jordanian part of Israel and Jews living on the Israeli side of the border were allowed no access whatsoever to this, one of their most sacred monuments. The issue was a long and bitter one between Israel and Jordan and led to numerous incidents, though subsequent events have changed the position. The labels are small and printed in only one colour on white paper, but they graphically portray the scene at the Wall as women crouch and stand before it to ' wail '.

A set of 12 labels showing historic buildings in Prague was issued in 1958, and as that was the year of the Universal & International Exhibition in Brussels the sets, attractively gift-

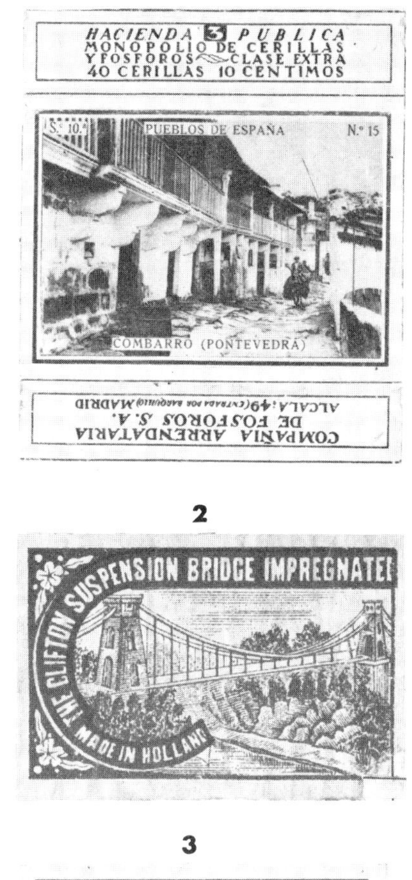

1. View of Spanish village from set of 35, c1936 2. Old Dutch label showing Brunel's Clifton Suspension Bridge, over the Avon Gorge, Bristol, England 3. View of beach and pier at Bournemouth, England, on Belgian label issued c1960 for a Bournemouth store

wrapped, were put on sale in the Czechoslovakian pavilion there. Simultaneously the set was issued in Prague for the home market. Those who bought the matches at the exhibition commented on the quality of the paper—thick and very white; but any who travelled on to Prague and bought the same labels there noticed that the paper used for home sales was much thinner

1

2

3

4

5

1. Typical red, white and blue American label 2. One of set of 12 views of Prague issued in Czechoslovakia, 1958 3. The old Turkish bridge at Mostar, Yugoslavia, issued for the home market 4. The famous Battle of Bunker Hill monument, another USA label 5. View of a famous street in New Orleans, USA

1. Issued for Tri-State Paper Co in USA 2. Rare old gold and pink label from Czechoslovakia for export to India 3. Yugoslavian advertising label issued in Cornwall, England, by the St Austell Brewery in the early 1960s, showing a dump of china-clay, the St Austell area's principal industry 4. Belgian label for export and sale in the Isle of Wight, England, 1963 5. Austrian label for Bolivia, publicising exports of petrol from the country in 1956

1

2

3

4

5

and off-white; just another example of the best being reserved for the shop window. One collector actually pointed out the difference when visiting a Czech match factory, but the comment received a cold reception!

Yugoslavia's Dolac factory at Sibica turns out matches intended for the home market, whilst the mighty Osijek plant copes with export orders as well and turns out a very different type of product. Yet the Dolac issues are the more interesting: although more crudely printed they have an unspoilt charm. Some reproductions of woodcuts showing famous features of Yugoslavia were issued a few years ago and never was the lovely old Turkish bridge at Mostar shown in better light than in the simply-printed design in red and green on white paper. So often the locally-issued product surpasses that intended for more sophisticated markets.

One of the finest sets ever produced came from J. John Masters Ltd who, a few years back, distributed a 'Cathedrals of Britain' set on 'drawing-room' box skillets; the firm also sold a 'Castles of Britain' series. The reverse carried a comprehensive description of the building pictured in the full-colour glossy photograph on the front. The only snag with these large, thick skillets is that they are bulky for storage, unless

1. Jamaica Inn, Bolventor, Cornwall, setting of Daphne du Maurier's novel of that name; from a set of 12 2. Czechoslovakian label showing hotel at Hammamet, one of several produced for the Tunisian Government, 1962 to publicise tourist resorts in Tunisia 3. Iceland's famous volcano Hekla on a Czechoslovakian label for export to Iceland, issued to US forces in the island during world war II 4. Good old Norwegian export label 5. Old Swedish export label 6. Monte Orgeuil Castle, Jersey, Channel Islands, floodlit at night; Czechoslovakian label

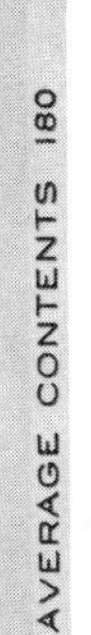

1

2

3

4

1. Handsome Swedish skillet, one of set of 12 produced for J. John Masters Ltd for sale in Britain and showing full-colour photographs and histories of British cathedrals 2. Belgian export label, c1936 3. Austrian label for export to India, c1900; the famous Qutb Minar Tower at Delhi 4. Norwegian export label c1929

one thins them by peeling off layers at the back; rather than do that and spoil a very fine cover many collectors will not keep them at all, thereby depriving themselves of interesting material.

Those responsible for the manufacture or marketing of matches are always striving after something with particular appeal to their own market, so 'The Old Cornish Mine' series could not fail to please when put on sale in Cornwall; in fact, they seemed to be so successful that they were sold in other parts of Britain as well. What the Cornishman, gloating over the full-colour picture of, for instance, the famous Dolcoath Mine at Camborne, cannot happily accept is that although the designs are drawn in Cornwall by a Cornish artist, the labels are actually printed in Russia to adorn boxes of Russian matches. The set, which is now current, will eventually contain 50 different labels, but despite the series title the designs include such far-from-mining subjects as the famous Jamaica Inn, the historic Falcon Hotel at Bude, and the replacing of the Logan Rock—an ancient balancing rock which was toppled by vandals in the late nineteenth century and had to be put back in position again if bad luck was not to befall the county.

With its wealth of historic and interesting monuments, Cornwall has had its fair share of label publicity and Jamaica Inn has had the distinction of appearing in another set, this time the 'Interesting Hotels' of Moreland's 'England's Glory' brand, although in this case full justice is hardly done to its attractions. The labels are printed only in dark blue on white paper and many of the photographs have the blurred quality of newspaper reproductions. Nevertheless, this set is much sought after by collectors, and the fact that it really only circulates in the West of England makes its acquisition all the more worthwhile.

It is impossible here to mention more than representative examples of the innumerable matchbox labels which have taken landmarks, world-famous buildings and monuments, etc, as their subject matter. They range from the Sphinx of Egypt (surprisingly pictured in one case on an old American label for the Diamond Match Co) to Iceland's volcano Hekla; from woodcuts of Italian classical sights to remote Spanish villages; and from St Paul's Cathedral, London to Pirates Alley, New Orleans. Yet the subject is rarely, if ever, adopted by collectors for specialisation.

8 *Marine Life*

1

2

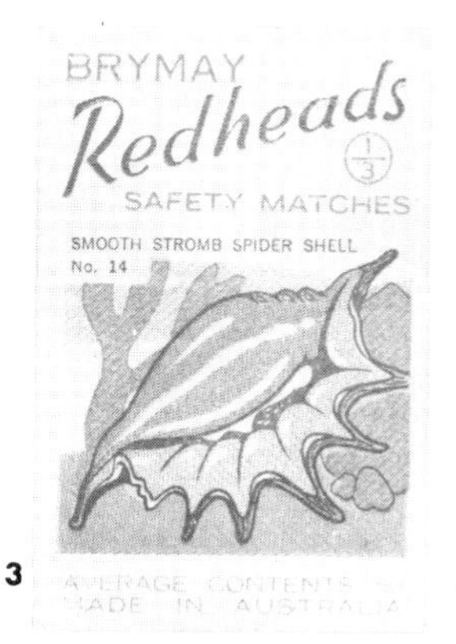

3

4

1. Seahorse and jellyfish on a modern Russian label from zoological set 2. Indian label 3. The smooth stromb spider shell in the Australian marine-life set 4. An early 'customer's' label from Russia

To SPEAK of a jellyfish on a matchbox label is rather like talking about a bird's nest in soup—no one quite believes you. But an Italian match manufacturer did issue a label in the early 1950s entitled 'Jellyfish', which showed one of those curious creatures floating along. An expert states that the jellyfish depicted is *Chrysaora isosceles*, whose sting can penetrate human skin and which has twenty-four long tentacles trailing from its margin. The drawing on the label appears to be correct in every detail; a lot can be learnt on a great variety of subjects through the humble medium of matchboxes.

Marine life has in fact come in for considerable attention from label designers. Fish especially have been portrayed by a number of countries, and lesser-known forms of marine life have not been forgotten. Italy was not the only country to feature a jellyfish; a fairly recent Russian set featured zoology, including a seahorse and a jellyfish on one label. These labels with their green background, no margin lines and clean-cut drawings are particularly attractive. The seahorse, that fascinating little fish with a prehensile tail and horse-shaped head, swimming vertically, so often seen in aquaria, is common in warm seas and in the Greek islands vast quantities are caught, dried and sold to tourists as souvenirs.

Societa Annonima Finanziaria Fiammiferi ed Affini (better known as SAFFA) of Milan, the giant Italian match concern which produced 'Jellyfish', also issued during the same period 'The Shark' and 'The Coral'. The former came in several variations of paper but again the drawing was masterfully executed. 'The Coral' is a most unusual picture. At first glance it might be difficult to recognise its subject, but closer inspection shows it to be an authentic-enough piece of red coral, the branched type which is much favoured for the fashioning of ornaments and jewellery.

A label printed in Macao also features coral, but in this instance a piece 'planted' in a pot which could be mistaken for a growing fern or even a piece of seaweed. This particular label, issued a few years ago, caused a mild rumpus when it was first distributed in the Far East. The matches are made by Cheung Ming Match Co of Macao but on the label was printed 'Made in

1

3

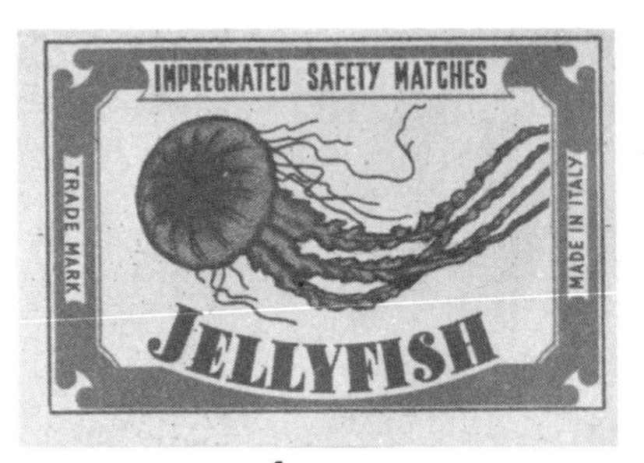

4

2

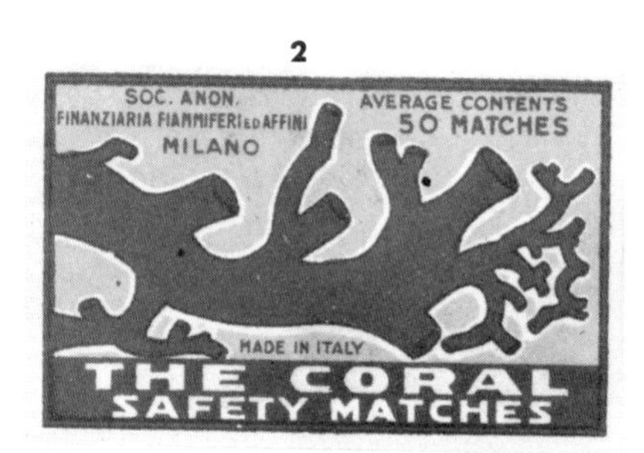

5

1, 2 & 4. Italian export labels of a few years ago 3. Australian fish from set of 64 showing Australian marine life 5. Belgian export label

1. Portuguese label 2. Coral shown on label from Macao 3. Conch shell from India 4. The Japanese carp, c1890 5. Modern Polish export label 6. Angel fish from India 7. Ceylon 8. From set of 3 fish from Communist China

China'. Macao is jealous of its independence of China and there the trouble arose; it never built up to an international incident but the labels had a short life.

Australia has perhaps made more use of marine life for matchbox labels than any other country. A 1965 set of 64 showed sea creatures from off the coast of Australia—fish, shells, the lot; a most interesting set, this was very popular with collectors. The matches on which the labels were used were Brymay 'Redheads'. Fish depicted on labels tend, as with animals and birds, to be those native to the area concerned. British labels are noticeably lacking in marine designs, perhaps because the creatures swimming in local waters are not sufficiently exotic to merit attention.

9 *Myth and Legend*

DOWN THE years myths and legends have played a big part in man's life. In these more sophisticated days they still fascinate him; here and there, notably in the Greek tourist industry, they have become big business. Match manufacturers too have exploited their potential, sometimes in quite a large way.

Though some people might not put it under the heading of myth, an old British label with the title 'Adam & Eve' deserves mention. Printed in light green on white paper, the trade mark a fig leaf, it was not arresting in appearance; but as it appeared at a time when simple humour was considered hardly dignified, its issue with the bold claim 'The First Match' printed on the box caused some annoyance among rival manufacturers—less at the play on words than because it could not claim to be the first match ever produced. One leading match manufacturer of the period threatened to bring legal action, but since the words could obviously be interpreted in various ways he had no firm case to bring and the matter fizzled out.

Of all the nursery-rhyme labels, those which have proved by far the most popular with collectors are the Swedish 'Nursery Land' ones.

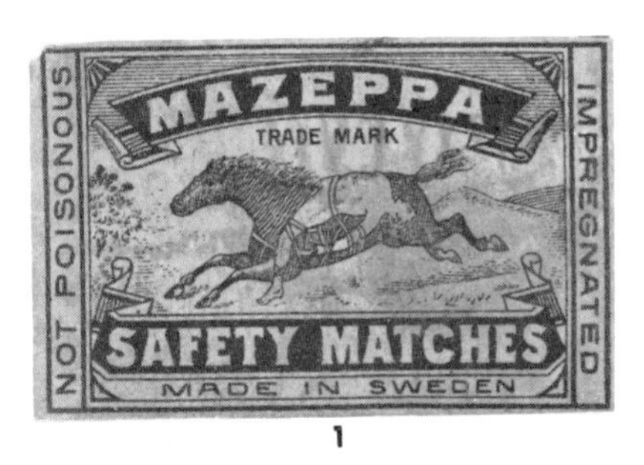

1

3

6

2

5

4

1. Swedish label commemorating a colourful figure in Russian legend 2. An early Japanese interpretation of a famous mythical character 3. Old Swedish label, now very scarce 4. Typical American label 5. Kali shown on Indian label 6. Scene from the story of Don Quixote, Spain

These were affixed to boxes of matches for export to English-speaking markets and they first appeared in England in 1902, selling at what even in those days must have been the incredibly low price of 1½d for a dozen boxes. The labels were issued in sets of 60 and 8 sets have been recorded, but no one is quite sure even now that that is the complete list. So esteemed were the labels among collectors and so keen has been the demand for them that in the 1930s and again in the 1950s some unscrupulous persons produced forgeries of them, and doubtless made a good deal of money from innocents willing to pay almost anything to complete a set. Yet these labels are not colourful or particularly prepossessing; they are, however, a product of Kreuger & Co, and Kreuger has always been a name with which to conjure in the match industry.

One of the initial attractions of the 'Nursery Land' set to collectors at the beginning of the century was probably that it carried the offer: 'If you collect and send F. Kreuger & Co Ltd, 10 Eastcheap, London EC a full set of all the 60 different Packet Labels of these matches they will mount them for you in a nice Album'. A free gift was always the advertising man's dream.

Even with 60 different 'Nursery Land' labels, some well-known rhymes are not included, but they have probably been used by other manufacturers at different times. 'Bo-Peep' has been one of the most popular brands in Northern Ireland for many years. Mother Hubbard going to the cupboard while her dog watches hopefully was the subject of the Belgian 'Mother Hubbard' matches of the 1930s, and about the same period or perhaps a little earlier Holland issued a similarly designed label (could it have been by the same artist?) for 'Jack & the Beanstalk' matches. 'The Three Bears' came from Belgium in the 1920s and rather curiously carried the information in Swedish that the matches were without phosphorus, although the rest of the wording on the label is in English. The drawing shows mother bear handing a slightly protesting baby bear over to father bear for safe keeping. Four medals shown on the label are presumably expected to pass as prize medals, but actually they are merely portraits of Kaiser Wilhelm II and Kaiser Frederick and their wives Augusta and Victoria of Prussia.

1

2

3

4

5

1. Ceres the corn goddess from the Australian mythological set, April 1963 2. Old Dutch export label 3. Japanese copy of a Russian label 4. The original Russian label 5. Old and scarce Belgian export label

In the realms of mythology matchbox labels have ranged far and wide. The figures of classical Greek mythology have been selected frequently, and such countries as China and India

Very rare old British all-round label

have concentrated on their own popular gods and goddesses. Once again Australia has been to the fore, releasing in April 1963 a set of 64 labels featuring mythological figures, each one being appropriately numbered in Roman figures.

The familiar stories of Hercules and Atlas have especially attracted the label designers. The Greek hero, Hercules, son of Jupiter and Alcmena, was celebrated for his prodigious bodily strength which enabled him to perform twelve labours of superhuman magnitude. Atlas, one of the Titans, was condemned to bear up the heavens with his head and hands. Finland issued 'Herkules' (sic) and the former Indo-China (now Vietnam) came up with 'Atlas', both figures shown in kneeling position and supporting the universe on their shoulders. A number of other countries selected the same design for labels, presumably to illustrate the powers of the matches contained in the boxes.

An interesting example of plagiarism is a label entitled 'Pandora'. This particular design first appeared from Russia in the early 1930s; printed in blue and red on white paper it showed the subject of the Greek myth who, according to Hesiod, was the first woman. She was supposed to have brought with her from heaven a box containing all human ills—or blessings—and on its being opened by her husband, Epimetheus, all escaped from it, leaving only Hope. The Russian label showed Pandora kneeling, the box open before her and two fairy-like figures flying from it. Some years later an almost identical Japanese label appeared on the market, printed in the same colours and with exactly the same sort of drawing of Pandora. It had the audacity to include under the title 'Pandora' the word 'Regd', printed exactly as it had been on the Russian label; in filching the design the Japanese manufacturer may well not have known what the inscription meant.

As a sidelight to the story, years after the original issue of the label, the writer was discussing with a Japanese collector the subject of Japan's habit of adopting other countries' label designs and 'Pandora' was mentioned. As quick as lightning he came up with the explanation that the Russian label had dealt with *one* version of the myth, which was that Pandora was sent by Zeus when the heavenly fire was stolen by Prometheus and that each of the gods gave her some gift hurtful to mankind; which, considering the connection between fire and matches, probably was in the mind of the designer. *But*, he said, the Japanese label dealt with the entirely

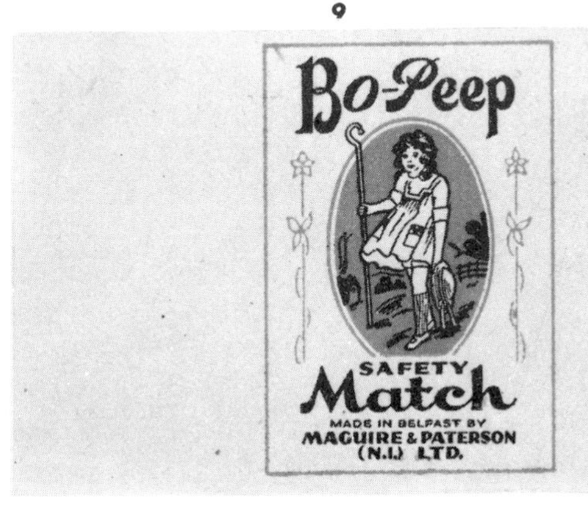

1. Dozen packet label illustrating an old Devonshire song 2. Old and scarce British label 3. Scarce label from the former Indo-China 4. Well-known Esthonian label of late 1930s 5. Russian label, c1900 6. From set of 3 labels depicting morning, noon and night from India 7. Finnish label for the home market 8. Finnish export label 9. Modern version of a long-standing Irish label design

different version that the celestials presented Pandora with a box full of winged blessings for men, but that on Pandora opening the box all except Hope flew away. There we left the subject!

Not quite so controversial is Finland's 'Juno' Impregnated Safety Match, an export brand of the 1930s when Finland was one of the foremost world exporters of matches. Juno, wife of Jupiter (Zeus), was identified with the Greek goddess, Hera; on the label she is shown in silhouette running over the top of the universe and brandishing a scroll, presumably conveying the good news in her role as goddess of marriage and births.

In earlier days Russia had a leaning towards mythology on labels for her extensive export market, and one of the best known of all Russian labels is 'Pegasus', which came in a series of endless variations. The trade mark was first registered in 1882 and was continued up to the 1930s. 'In the old days Pegasus symbolised the lightning and thunder carrier in the heavens. Today it symbolises the lightning striker as produced by "Pegasus Brand Safety Matches"' is the information given on a reverse label which was affixed to Pegasus boxes sent to Britain in the early part of this century. In Greek mythology Pegasus was of course the winged steed who sprang from the blood of Medusa and who belonged to Apollo and the Muses. With a blow of his hoofs he produced the fountain Hippocrene or Helicon, whence poets drew their inspiration. This is a little different from the matchbox version of the fable, but the latter of course suited the purpose better!

As would be expected, national symbols have duly featured on matchbox labels, notably those two stalwarts—John Bull and Uncle Sam. The latter is the popular designation for the initials US, and is generally depicted as a bearded old gentleman with a tall hat. The origin of John Bull is less easily explained; he is supposedly the English people personified, or a typical Englishman, but was the typical Englishman ever a rotund figure with sidewhiskers and flat hat? Be that as it may, Morelands of Gloucester formerly used John Bull as the trade mark for its 'England's Glory' brand and also later marketed a 'John Bull' brand. 'Uncle Sam' is the title of what are described as 'Safety Strike on Box Matches' produced many years ago by the Diamond Match Co of USA, the label being printed in the familiar red, white and blue which typifies US labels. In this design he is wearing a coat decorated with stars, and trousers with stripes, and is holding a scroll (presumably the Declaration of Independence); in a Dutch version of an 'Uncle Sam' brand of the 1900s he is shown head and shoulders only and with his tall hat emblazoned with stars and stripes.

Legendary figures of literature and song have played their part on matchbox labels. Spain has naturally always been associated with Don Quixote and in the 1940s Cervantes SA appropriately selected scenes from *Don Quixote* to illustrate the front panels of some all-round-the-box labels which carried, on the reverse, slogans advertising insurance. The Canary Islands also chose Don Quixote for an all-round label, and there a silhouette drawing on the reverse panel shows the hero and his faithful retainer mounting a hill on their tired steeds after tilting at a windmill.

Sir James Barrie's immortal Peter Pan has given his name to a Swedish label of the 1920s, but whether the drawing represents the collector's idea of Peter depends upon which version of the stage play he has seen. Another Swedish label of some years ago recorded a less-known legend. Called 'Mazeppa', it showed a naked man strapped to a horse in full gallop. In the later seventeenth century a Pole, Ivan Stephanovitch Mazeppa Koledinsky, a page in the court of the King of Poland, was caught while having an intrigue with a nobleman's wife. The furious husband had him stripped and tied to the back of a wild horse, which was then driven out into the bleak Russian desert. But Mazeppa was released by a band of roving Cossacks, and survived to lead a prominent and adventurous life, dying in 1709 at the age of sixty-five.

A recent (1967) British label issued by the Two Counties Match Co of Honiton, Devon, another in a series of 50, shows in full colour 'Old Uncle Tom Cobley and All' on their epic ride from Widecombe on the old grey mare. But if that is Widecombe church nestling in the hollow, why is the signpost to Widecombe pointing in the opposite direction?

Japan and China have made most use of their own rich mythology on matchbox labels. Other countries, especially India, have turned to it as well, and a great many export labels from Sweden, Austria, etc, featured Hindu gods and goddesses, as they were certain bestsellers on the markets for which they were destined. China, too, used them prior to the revolution which produced Communist China; such designs are now frowned upon.

Indian mythology is involved and complicated with lengthy stories attached to every figure por-

1

2

3

4

5

6

7

1. Swedish fairytale set of 5, issued 1948 2. British, issued 1905 3. Don Quixote from the Canary Islands 4. Indian elephant god Ganesa on an old Japanese label for export to India 5. Belgian export label of the late 1930s 6. A 'customer's' label from USA 7. Greek mythology on an old Belgian label

trayed. From 1880 until the 1920s Japan exported to India a large quantity of labels bearing designs drawn from mythology, the Divine Triad of Brahma, Vishnu and Siva being the favourite subject. One of the most popular of Hindu divinities is Ganesa, who appears on a great many Indian labels. He was made by Parvati from the dew of her body mingled with dust, and acts as guardian to the goddess's gate. Small and stocky, he is always portrayed as holding in his four arms an elephant-goad, a rosary and an alms bowl.

The Indian conception of demons has many aspects and one of the most horrible and most venerated was Kali, shown on a variety of labels from India. Among her unpleasant achievements is that of drinking the blood of an adversary in order that each drop which fell from his body should not give birth to a thousand giants. Kali is always represented with a very dark complexion, long loose hair and four arms. To complete the macabre picture her ear-rings are two corpses and she wears a necklace of human skulls. A charming design indeed for a matchbox label—but a best-seller in India.

The most famous and perhaps the most apt of all mythological names associated with matches is not just a brand name, but has been given to matches themselves and has remained in common use to this day in the match industry. Vesta, the Roman goddess of virginity, of fire and of the domestic hearth, gave her name to the improved matches which followed the rather crude Congreve; the 'new' match with stems of untwisted cotton threads covered with wax, named after the goddess in whose temple the sacred fire perpetually burned. To this day wax vestas are manufactured in some countries, although their popularity is steadily diminishing. The name will not be forgotten and it is surely fitting that one of the world's greatest mythological figures should be remembered in one of man's simplest but most far-reaching and valuable inventions.

10 *Occupations*

No MATTER what your profession or trade, it is more than likely that it has at some time been recorded on a matchbox label, with the artist's impression of a 'typical' representative of the particular occupation. Midshipman to matador, and fisherman to farmer, have all been lined up; modern titles have included porter, tea girl, driver, airman, mechanic. Yet despite the variety offered, not many collectors specialise in this group.

The dress of the people depicted on occupations labels is not always an indication of the period of issue, as in some cases the artist has taken his inspiration from years gone by and not from his own days. For instance 'Farmer' was a Finnish export brand popular during the late 1920s and early 1930s, but even forty or fifty years ago the farmer did not carry out his tasks dressed in high hat and smock—the old conception of the dress of one who worked on the land.

The sea has had a particular fascination for designers of labels featuring occupations; we have 'Admiral' from Norway and Sweden, 'Commodore' from Czechoslovakia, 'Fisherman' from Belgium, 'Nationals Sailor' from India (a puzzling title), 'Pilot' also from India, 'Midshipman' from Russia and so on. Outdoor work on the land has appealed too, as witness 'Farmer' from Finland, 'Woodman' also from Finland, 'Shepherd' from Norway, and others.

The world of entertainment is duly recognised in its many varying branches. 'The Clown' from Belgium comes in a great many varieties; Sweden has sold 'Matador' with a dramatic drawing of the controversial Spanish spectacle of

1

2

3

4

5

6

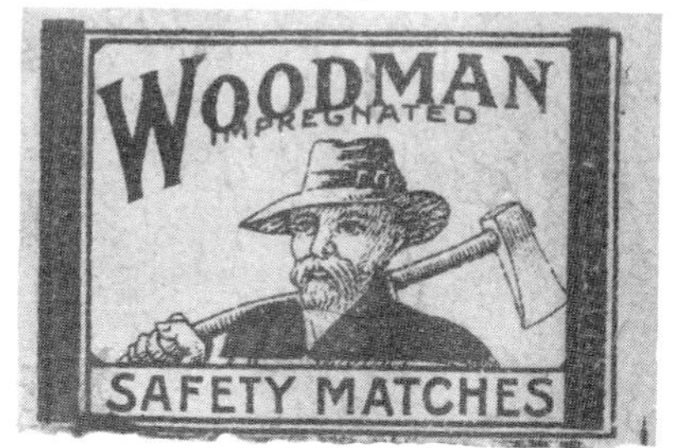

7

8

9

10

11

12

1. Recent Czechoslovakian export label 2. Rare old Norwegian label 3. Russian, early 1930s 4. Early Japanese label 5. Scarce old Norwegian label 6. Latvia, pre-1939 7. Modern label from Singapore 8. One variety of a well-known Belgian label of the 1930s 9. Old Dutch label 10 & 11. Indian labels 12. Rare blue and white variety of a well-known label issued 1920s and 30s

bullfighting. It was Japan, of course, which produced 'The Geisha', a multi-coloured head-and-shoulders picture of the young lady whom the dictionary tersely describes as 'a Japanese dancing girl', but whom an American magazine has more recently dubbed 'the girl who offers the entire field of entertainment for the tired business man'. The geishas are of course genuinely much more than dancing girls, and can provide such varied diversions as the Japanese tea ceremony, light and amusing conversation, musical performances and so on, though at what is now a very stiff charge, the rates being fixed by their 'trade union'. Indian and Austrian labels portray dancing girls and another Indian design shows a man holding a mask in front of his face, entitled 'Comic'.

'Smithy' from Russia shows something no longer familiar to all, a smith working at the anvil fashioning a horseshoe. The set of chimney brushes shown on the Belgian 'Sweep' labels is also less frequently seen in these days of vacuum chimney cleaning; and the collier shown kneeling and holding a pick on a popular Belgian label of the 1930s recalls the days before the mechanisation of coal mining.

The popularity of 'occupation' designs seems to be fading; possibly the picturesque appeal of too many jobs has disappeared with ubiquitous and standardised mechanisation. Clothes worn for everyday work are much the same everywhere, and good subjects for interesting designs are difficult to find.

The modern soldier, too, has been standard-

1

2

3

4

5

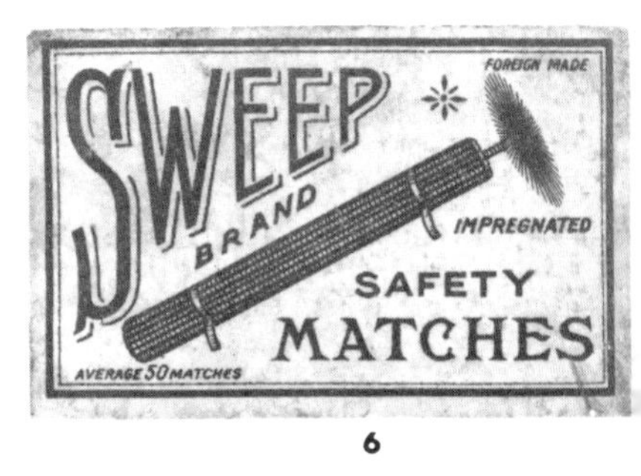

6

1. Old-fashioned farmer from Finland; export label 2. Good early Swedish label for large-size box containing 95 matches 3. Old Swedish export label 4. Czechoslovakian, c1911 5. Modern Indian label 6. Popular Belgian export brand of the 1930s

ised in dress, but here some relics of pageantry and colour can be found. Not long ago a brightly coloured label from Singapore entitled 'Lifeguard' appeared on the market in that city, bearing a head-and-shoulders drawing of a member of Britain's Household Cavalry in full dress uniform. Technical details are probably not entirely accurate, but the design is effective. Another army label, but less spectacular, is the 'Ypres Best Tommy Safety Match' issued in Belgium at the end of world war I. Printed in drab shades it shows a British soldier sitting on rubble amid the ruins of a shell-shattered town, nonchalantly smoking a cigarette.

11 Personalities

In this field the choice of subjects for label designers is literally limitless and people both famous and obscure, from the early days of the household match until the present, have been honoured by a place on a matchbox. Naturally each country's manufacturers have tended to feature their own national heroes—heroines have been conspicuous by their absence.

Just a few women have achieved commemoration, those selected representing widely varying fields of activity. Lady Curzon appeared in a medallion portrait next to that of her husband on an old Swedish label when Lord Curzon became Britain's Viceroy of India. Russia's first woman in space was shown in a short series of labels honouring the USSR astronauts, including the most famous one of all, Yuri Gagarin. It took an unlikely country like Iran (then Persia) to commemorate one of the Western world's best-known personalities of the 1930s, America's child film-star Shirley Temple. The Persian label provided an excellent photograph, but throughout her meteoric career Shirley never appeared on a label from any other source.

1

2

3

4

1. Japanese Admiral Togo and General Oyama of the Russo-Japanese war 2. Sebastian Cabot, issued 1911 3. Mahatma Gandhi on an Indian label 4. Simon Bolivar; Swedish label for export to Venezuela

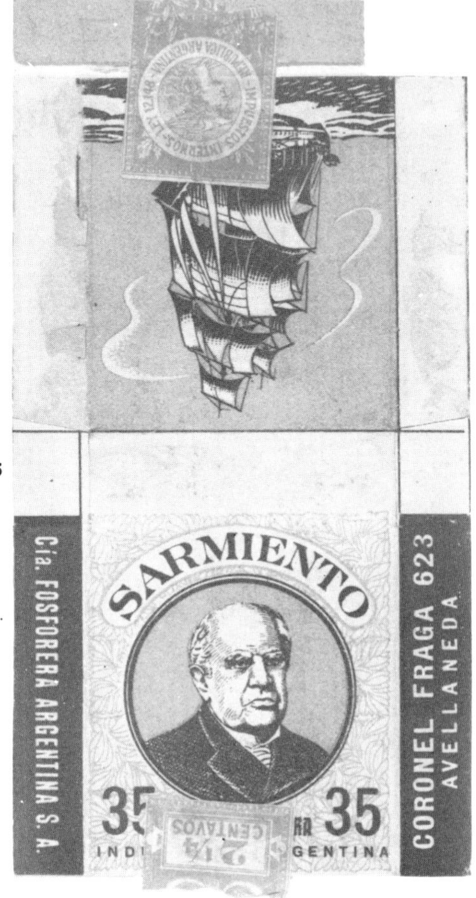

1. Glazed Japanese label for export to India from a set of 6, showing the Maharajah of Baroda 2. Modern Hungarian label commemorating bacteriologist Robert Koch 3. President Nasser of Egypt on a label from Hong Kong, 1956 4. Vasco da Gama on a recent Portuguese label 5. Sarmiento, Argentinian liberal reformer

Iranian matchboxes are, incidentally, smaller than those from most other countries, and the labels therefore readily recognisable. For many years Iran had an ill-organised 'cottage' type match industry, attempts to establish it going back to 1904. In those early days, and in fact for many years, crude phosphorus was obtained by burning bones, and for the making of the matchsticks thin sheets were shaved from green wood by hand-operated machines. Nowadays the industry is comparatively up-to-date, although hemmed in by State control.

Many of the bewildering variety of famous men shown on labels are political celebrities, men to whom their countries wished to show gratitude. Guiseppe Garibaldi (1807-82) the great Italian patriot and national liberator, is shown on an early Italian label wearing his famous red shirt, sitting astride his horse and brandishing a sword. Louis Kossuth (1802-94), who performed a similar service for Hungary, features on a Hungarian label of about the same period and is shown in a head-and-shoulders portrait; the label is printed in the Hungarian national colours of red and green on white.

In the nineteenth century Italy was particularly active in portraying other countries' national leaders, many of these labels being very fine designs. One example, belonging to a short set which is extremely rare today, depicts Napoleon (1769-1821), Emperor of France: the portrait is set in a medallion. Italy also featured

Karl Marx (1818-83) on one of the few labels issued outside Russia to show that controversial figure. In fact that label should really be included in this book's 'Propaganda' chapter, as it was issued by the Socialist party of the Adriatic provinces of Italy at the turn of the century and faithfully exhorts the workers to unite. Marx, however, deserves mention in his own right as a colourful and vastly influential personality.

Spain was another country which in the last century was much given to adorning its matchboxes with pictures of famous men from other countries. One of the best photographs of Abraham Lincoln (1809-65), sixteenth President of the United States, was reproduced on a rare Spanish label printed in Barcelona about 1889. A tribute to the quality of the printing of these early Spanish labels—great favourites with collectors and keenly sought—is that although they have mostly yellowed slightly with age, something virtually unavoidable with photographic labels, however carefully they are stored, the portraits are as clear today as when they were first published.

Leaving political subjects for the field of discovery, it is to be expected that Australia should have honoured Captain James Cook (1728-79), whose three famous voyages still stir the imagination of every schoolboy. Following his successful circumnavigation of the globe, he made his epic voyage to the southern hemisphere in 1772. His last voyage began in July 1776 and he was killed in Hawaii in 1779. 'Captain Cook

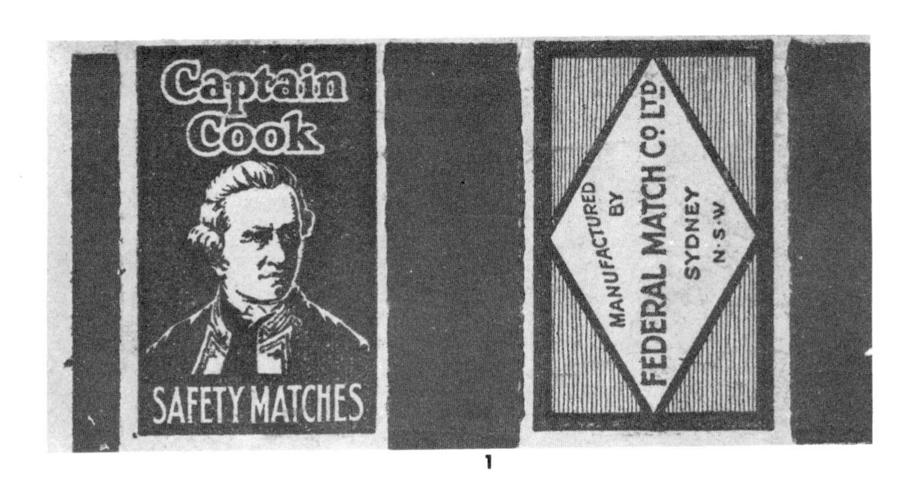

1. Famous Australian all-round label of some years ago 2. Cricketer Denis Compton pictured at the height of his career in a set of Australian portraits of cricketers

Early British label

1. C. S. Parnell and J. E. Redmond on an old Irish label 2 & 3. British labels issued at the time of the Boer War showing Lord Kitchener and General Smuts

1

2

3

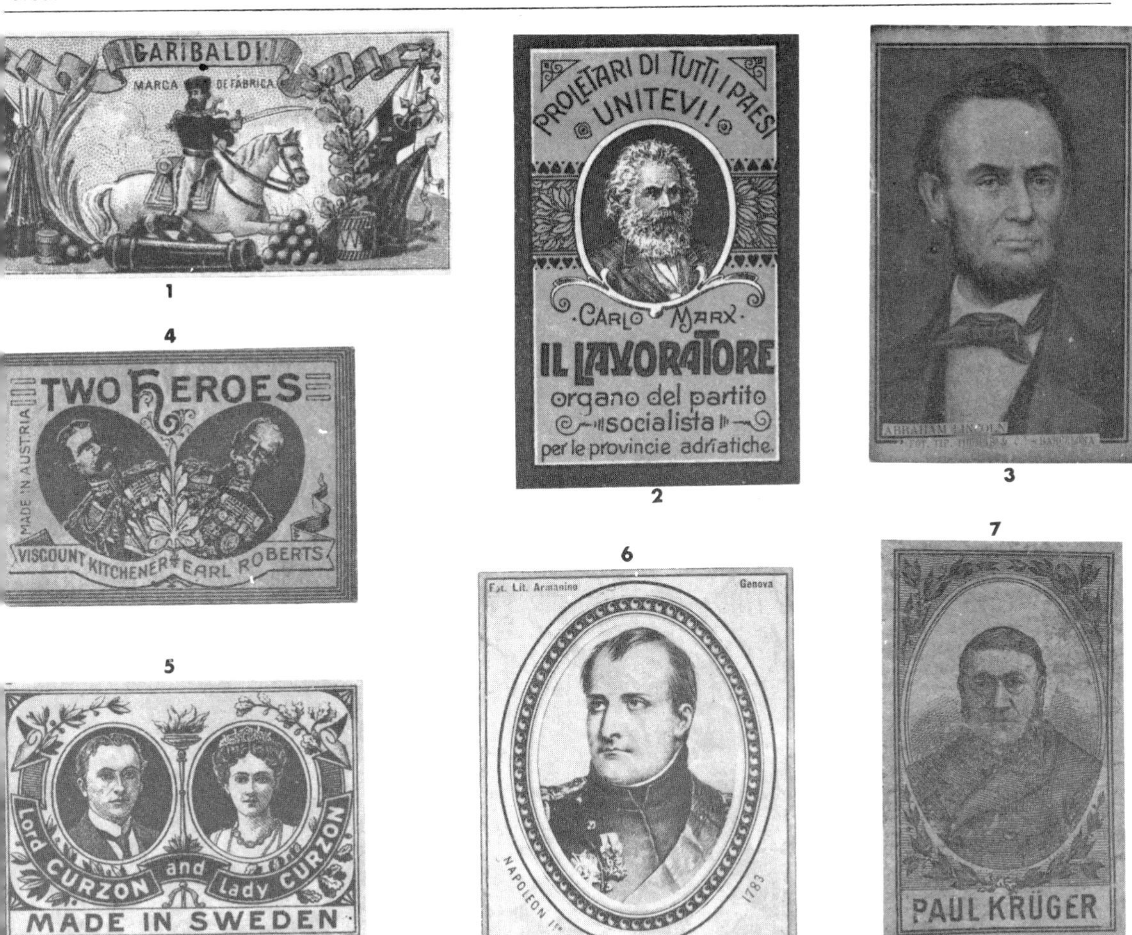

1. Issued to commemorate 50th anniversary of death of Garibaldi 2. Karl Marx on an Italian label exhorting people of the Adriatic provinces to unite 3. Abraham Lincoln shown on an early and rare Spanish label 4. Viscount Kitchener and Earl Roberts on an Austrian label issued during the Boer War 5. Lord and Lady Curzon when Viceroy and Vicereine of India 6. Old Italian label picturing Napoleon 7. Rare old Dutch label showing Paul Krüger, President of the Transvaal Republic 1881-1900

Safety Matches' by the Australian Federal Match Co were a favourite brand 'down under' for a great many years, although when first introduced they did not sell well. In 1928 there was no import duty on matches in Australia and the market became a dumping ground for cheap products from Russia, Japan, China, etc, retailing at 3½d or 4d per dozen boxes. At first the matches sold readily but they were not dampproof and in wet weather and humid conditions the heads fell off. Sales of the better-quality Federal matches began to improve, but children who had been collecting the many colourful labels from other countries were disappointed when they were withdrawn, leaving only one Federal design. As a result of their outcry, Federal decided to boost sales by issuing a new label each month and to feature educational subjects. Captain Cook was on the first one issued and it was planned to follow with a picture of his ship *Endeavour* and then a portrait of Captain Philip, the first Governor of Australia. However, when 'Captain Cook' appeared sales dropped instead of rising and plans to continue the series were scrapped. But over the years 'Captain Cook' became far more popular until it finally achieved bestseller status.

The old Bristol Match Co chose to honour English navigator Sebastian Cabot (1475-1557) on a cleverly designed label printed in red, white and blue, on which the 'Cabot Match' was designated 'Bristol's Pioneer'—in honour o both the matches and of Cabot. Although Cabo lived so long ago and the 'Cabot Match' wa first issued in 1911, at first glance the drawin could be taken as showing a modern space man

1

2

1. Sir Walter Scott and 'The Lady of the Lake' on a rare old British label c1885 2. General McMahon, French soldier of Irish descent (1802-73) shown on an old British label c1873

ot until a few years ago did Portugal honour great explorer Vasco de Gama, on a label owing him as a venerable old gentleman not sily associated with outstanding exploits.

The long-defunct firm of Mitchell & Co, of ovan, Scotland, issued about 1885 what was en described as 'a revelation in matchbox bel design' (and that in the days before extravant television and press advertising). The label as certainly ornate and imposing, being an allund-the-box type for the deep, square-shaped oxes which were in use at the time. The front nel proclaimed 'Loch Katrine Matches' and d a large drawing of Sir Walter Scott, and the verse carried what was described as 'a drama- representation of the Lady of the Lake', plus verse from Scott's famous poem of that name. ions and Scotch thistles completed the design. he story goes that one of the boxes was even ut before Queen Victoria, who was treated to appropriate eulogy on it, but that the great dy's reaction was of the famous 'We are not nused' variety. Nowadays that label is a conoisseur's dream and not a great many copies ave remained intact. It is a great sadness to llectors to see these fine old all-round-the-box bels mutilated by being cut into separate nels, but unfortunately that is often done day.

The early British factories probably produced ore 'personality' labels than have ever been sued by any one country since, just as they elighted in illustrating events of the day. Gladone and other contemporary political figures, e explorers Stanley and Livingstone, Samuel imsoll (promoter of the Merchant Shipping ct of 1876), Charles Darwin, General IcMahon of France, Irish statesmen such as harles Parnell and Allen O'Brien, all had their xtra moment of fame, on labels marketed by ne or other of the now long-dead British match anufacturers such as Palmer, Barber, Seanor, sborne, etc.

The last decade has brought a movement toards renewed popularity for 'personality' bels, although not in Britain. Other countries ave spread their nets wide in the search for itable persons. In 1956, at the time of the verthrow of King Farouk of Egypt and the rise of General Nasser, a small label was printed in Hong Kong for matches exported to Egypt; the brand was entitled 'Premier Safety Matches', bearing on the label a likeness of General Nasser, although not a very flattering one.

Argentina is one of the countries still using wax matches sold in cardboard 'pull out' boxes, and a few years ago a skillet cover issue by the Cia Fosforera, Argentina SA, carried a portrait of Sarmiento, a great Argentinian liberal reformer who hated the gauchos. Hungary recently honoured German bacteriologist Robert Koch (1843-1910).

Japan and Austria at one time specialised in producing highly coloured glazed labels for export matches to India featuring portraits of Indian rulers. These were issued in sets, usually of 6, and are very popular with collectors today. The Russo-Japanese war of 1904, over the occupation of Korea, brought forth a spate of labels, mainly from Japan but also including a set from Sweden, portraying leading naval and military figures of both sides. This set is another classic among collectors.

Great names in sport have figured prominently and continue to be good sellers; Australia's sets of photographs of cricketers on the distinctive black and green all-round-the-box labels for Duncan's '60's Safety Matches' a few years ago are a supreme example of such popularity. A more unusual sporting personality was commemorated on a label from Belgium many years ago. In the IVth Olympic Games, held in London in 1908, the first competitor to cross the finishing line in the marathon event was Dorando Pietri of Italy who had completed the course from Windsor to Shepherds Bush, London. But during the last lap he became almost exhausted and received assistance from some track officials. This resulted in his disqualification and the winner was announced as John Hayes of America. But Dorando's plucky effort had brought acclaim and there was such a public outcry that a gold cup was later presented to him as a consolation award. 'Dorando A Match for All' was another outcome of the occasion, and the label shows the determined little Italian in full stride. It is printed in two shades of green on white paper, and not of particularly impres-

1. Olympic marathon runner Dorando, c1908 2. Danish label honouring explorer Tordenskjold 3. One of set of 6 Austrian glazed and highly coloured labels for export to India, early 1900s 4. A long-standing Belgian brand shows William Tell and his son 5 & 6. Russia's first man in space, Yuri Gagarin 7. One of several old Swedish labels featuring Napoleon 8. Swedish label for export to India 9. Admiral Lord Nelson as an inn sign on a set of modern labels issued by a well-known south of England tobacconist's firm 10. One of several varieties from Sweden showing General Gordon 11. Hungarian patriot Louis Kossuth on an old Hungarian label 12. Former child film-star Shirley Temple on label from Iran

sive appearance.

Some of the personalities from every walk of life who have been pictured on matchbox labels have now been forgotten by the general public, though all had their moment of fame. To the label collector they still live on, with Dorando sometimes taking precedence over Gandhi when it comes to exchanges, and younger collectors clamouring for a so-far overlooked subject—the Beatles.

12 *Propaganda*

For anyone wishing to propagate tenets, doctrines or systems, the ordinary matchbox, constantly handled by everyone, rich or poor, is an obvious medium for disseminating information. Even the most illiterate members of the world's population can understand the meaning of a picture, and on many propaganda labels there is no need for words.

The subjects used on propaganda labels cover a wide field—win the war, elect so and so, grow more food, work harder, learn to read and write, understand the dangers of disease, stamp out the Colorado beetle, drink more milk. Even the population explosion has been made the subject of such a label: at the end of 1966, making what was considered an innovation in this form of advertising, the Kerala State Government in India purchased space on matchboxes to publicise its family-planning campaign.

So many propaganda labels have been issued that some collectors specialise in them exclusively; and their collections can never be complete, for every day new issues are pouring forth, most especially from Russia and its satellite countries of eastern Europe, as well as Communist China and Yugoslavia; for all the Communist countries have long been aware of the potentialities of this form of indoctrination.

It is often difficult to draw a dividing line between propaganda labels and commemorative ones since frequently the two are combined to serve the same purpose. We have an example in the small-size label printed in Hong Kong with a picture of Mr Julius Nyerere, president of the recently-independent Tanzania: it was at the same time a recognition of Mr Nyerere's rise to power and a reminder to the population to continue to support him. Incidentally, Hong Kong seems to have specialised in the manufacture of such portrait labels; the one showing President

1

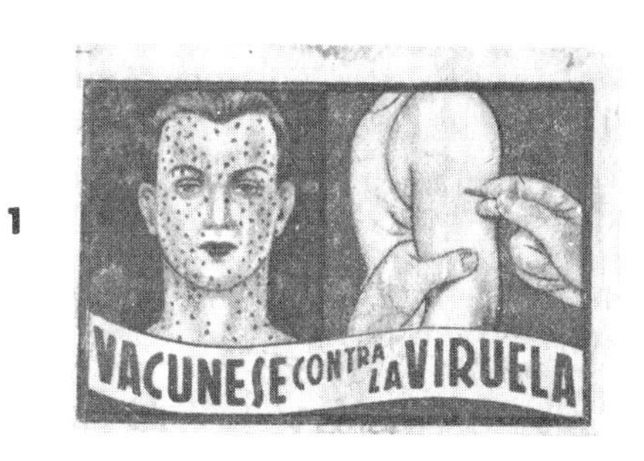

2

1. Italian propaganda for vaccination against smallpox 2. Italian world war II label with exhortation to dig and fight for victory

1. One of the famous Japanese propaganda labels 2. Polish warning against the Colorado beetle 3. Indian label for Mauritius 4. Italian literacy propaganda 5. One of set of 31 road-safety labels from Israel 6. 'Free India' propaganda 7. Anti-alcohol propaganda, Holland 8. German wartime warning against careless talk 9. East German warning about fire risks at harvest time 10. Drink more wine propaganda, France

Nasser of Egypt was mentioned in the last chapter. The same narrow borderline divides propaganda and advertising labels, for a label design may advertise goods whilst at the same time offering thinly-veiled comment on conditions of work or even on a political situation.

To the collector by far the most famous propaganda labels are those known now simply as 'the Japanese propaganda labels'; it is a measure of their fame that this description instantly identifies them. Fairly colourful but unattractive, they first appeared on boxes in the

Far East in 1942 and were the only ones available in Singapore when the British forces arrived there. Twenty-four different varieties are known to exist, a further 8 are believed to have existed, and they were numbered apparently haphazardly from 3 to 211; it is the numbering which most puzzles collectors, because there appears to be no logical continuity or progression. The labels depicted graphically the crushing of the Allied forces, and captions included 'Sure we must win', 'The Japanese army will gain the victory', and 'Strength of Asia'. One, with the true Japanese salesman's eye, even advised 'Collect labels of these matches'. And nowadays collectors almost literally scramble for them. The labels were also affixed to boxes of matches distributed in Malaya, Siam and Java; two of the designs circulated only in Java.

Of far more benevolent intent are the many national appeals which have been supported by S. J. Moreland & Son Ltd on the reverse panels of its 'England's Glory' brand, though these too were used during world war II as a contribution to the war effort: slogans such as 'Dig for Victory' and 'Save Fuel for Battle' were published. In peacetime Morelands has supported National Savings, road safety and so on. The second world war naturally brought forth a spate of propaganda labels from many countries. In Britain all the leading match manufacturers amended their labels accordingly and Bryant & May's 'Use Matches sparingly' and J. John Masters' 'Matches are Scarce, make them last' are now viewed with interest and a little wonder by the younger generation of collectors. Several countries—on both sides—adopted Winston Churchill's famous 'V for Victory' sign.

South Africa's 'Don't Talk about Ships' was one of the more unusual wartime labels; in Germany the warning was given more subtly with a label showing a shadowy 'cloak and dagger' figure on the prowl and the one word of warning 'Pst!' There was some conjecture at the time as to whether the figure was in-

1. East German label warning against forest fires 2. One from modern Rumanian set for reafforestation 3. Modern Czechoslovakian 'waste not, want not' slogan 4. Label from Swiss accident-prevention set of 25 5. Old Japanese export label 6. Pre-1939 Czechoslovakian nationalist propaganda 7. Modern Hungarian label advocating the growing of more cereals

1. Modern Israeli tourist propaganda 2. Russian commemoration of the Revolution 3. US label for export to Venezuela—stamp out germs 4. Scarce US all-round label of world war II, for distribution to the troops at Fort Oglethorpe only 5. Well-known Australian all-round label warning against bush fires 6. World war II Australian label 7. Polish wartime propaganda

tended to represent Churchill or Roosevelt, but in fact it was not designed as any particular individual. Careless talk in wartime was indeed a subject which many match manufacturers adopted. And during the Russo-Finnish war of the late 1940s, a graphic Finnish label for the home market showed a face with the lips padlocked together.

Czechoslovakia churns out so many propaganda labels on themes ranging from May Day commemoration to the pollution of rivers that it is difficult to keep pace with them. One of the more unusual sets issued a few years ago comprised 57 labels, each showing a scaled-down photograph of the front page of a newspaper, and all aimed at publicising newspapers with a purely Russian angle in their news and comments. The eastern part of Europe has always made great use of the propaganda label. The carve-up of the Austro-Hungarian empire brought forth many triumphant offerings. In 1918 there appeared in Slovakia a label which could be classed as either commemorative or propaganda. The design was of the Slovakian tricolour flag combined with the then provisional escutcheon of the new Czechoslovakia, which was composed of two shields with the Silesian and Moravian eagles set beneath the Slovakian double white cross on a red field, together with a sentence which translated as 'Hey Slovakia, still our Slovakian language lives'. These words were the opening ones of a song which originated in the days of revolution against the Austro-Hungarian monarchy in 1848 and which was composed by the Slovakian politician, Ludevit Stur.

Elections have long been a target for propaganda matchbox labels. At the time of the Saar plebisite in 1938 an effective black, red and white label urged voters to put their cross in the 'right' place and even the most illiterate could not fail to get the message. The United States of America, home of the bookmatch, where boxes of matches are the exception rather than the rule, has provided a skillet, printed in orange and black on a glossy white surface, which exhorts voters to 'Elect Donald A. Jones Macon County Judge' and adds the information that Mr Jones is a Democratic candidate. The election took place on 6 November 1962. These modern American advertising and propaganda boxes, shallower than the normal box, are of course produced at the expense of the candidate, and are printed to his personal order by the Diamond Match Div of America.

Of recent years many countries have issued sets of labels disseminating road-safety and accident-prevention propaganda; Russia, Hungary, Czechoslovakia and other Communist countries as well as Great Britain and the USA have done so, and in 1957 the Usego Corporation of Switzerland issued a set of 25 accident-prevention labels to which interest was added by linking them to a competition offering 300 prizes. In the same year Israel issued a set of 31 road-safety labels, as modern in design and concept, as was the Swiss set.

Among the countless other social problems illustrated on labels is that of illiteracy. Italy printed a label for boxes of matches being exported to South America which pointed out to the natives the advantages of literacy; the design showed a woman teaching a man to read from a simple illustrated book, emphasising the contribution which inhabitants can make to their own villages if they are able to read and write.

'France Toujours' proclaimed a label from the WIMCO factory on boxes of matches distributed in Mauritius. The design shows a Spahi astride his horse and holding aloft a pennant, but the reason for the patriotic outburst is obscure as there is no other wording on the label. Japan, quick to notice other countries' national problems, provided 'Home Rule' matches for export to Ireland earlier this century.

1

2

1. Rare old Yugoslavian label issued in Dalmatia
2. South African world war II slogan

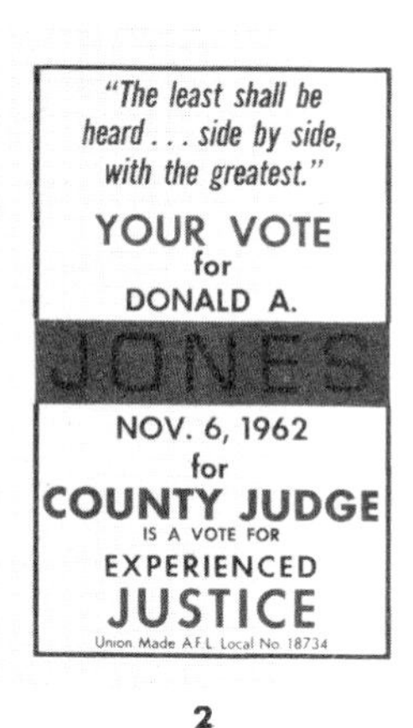

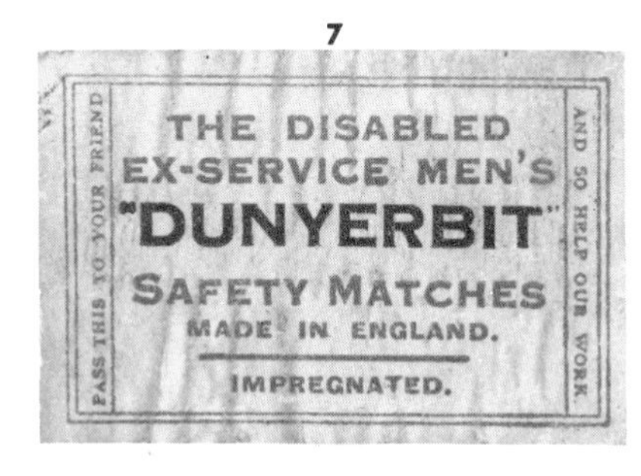

1. India, c1943 2. USA election skillet 3. Tanganyika freedom propaganda, 1963 4. Mr Jomo Kenyatta, President of Kenya, on Kenyan label 5. Indian political propaganda 6. Mr Julius Nyerere, President of Tanzania, on label from Hong Kong 7 & 8. British labels for matches made by disabled ex-servicemen after world war I 9. Czechoslovakian label for export to Africa, advocating African independence

Countries which have large areas of forest are naturally concerned about the fire risk and so we find warnings about the danger of fire figuring prominently among propaganda labels. Australia has used these freely, and such slogans as 'Prevent Bush Fires—Put Out Your Match' are commonplace on both all-round-the-box and single top labels from 'down under'. Some European countries advocate forest conservation by way of matchbox-label propaganda and a set of 12 labels from Rumania includes one urging re-afforestation and showing two young people planting saplings.

Yet another subject is the fight against disease, and a few years ago the Diamond Match Co of USA produced an export label for Venezuela showing a heavy boot crushing germs underfoot.

In a lighter vein, tourist propaganda—as an alternative to the pictures of beauty spots discussed in Chapter 7—features on labels from

1 & 3. English propaganda labels of world war II 2. Communist China 4. Rumanian productivity propaganda, late 1940s 5. Britain's famous 'Matches are precious—make them last' label during world war II 6. Modern Hungarian saving-scheme propaganda

some countries which are bent on developing their tourist trade. A 1966 set from Israel featured various holiday attractions, including swimming and other water sports, but the labels were rather crudely printed in red, white and blue and cannot have had much appeal to potential tourists in more affluent countries; as the wording is all in Hebrew, they were presumably intended for home sale only.

Holland has long faced the problems of alcoholism, perhaps not so acute now as it was some years ago, and this has provided the theme for several sets of matchbox labels distributed within the country since world war II. The first of these warning against insobriety appeared on labels as much as fifty years ago. It was in 1952-3 that 8 of what are known as the XP sets appeared, printed either in blue on white paper or in dark blue on light blue paper; they push such slogans as 'Eat more fruit, drink less alcohol'. In complete contrast France is all for encouraging the sale of wine, and a set of labels issued a few years ago by the National Committee for Propaganda in Support of Wine recommended wine-drinking. The tops of the labels carry the regulation red and white Safety Matches design of the state match monopoly SEITA, and the pictures beneath all show jolly-looking people imbibing or about to imbibe their wine. A favourite slogan on the labels is 'A meal without wine is a day without sun'.

Anticipation of the next subject to be used for a propaganda label from somewhere around the globe is a constant source of interest to label collectors.

13 Royalty

1

2

3

4

1. King Baudouin of the Belgians, one of a modern set showing members of the Belgian royal family 2. The Shah of Persia on a modern label 3. Emperor Franz Josef of Austria on an old Austrian label 4. King Gustav of Sweden, one of set of 6 from Austria, early 1900s

HERE WE have one of the most popular of all groups of labels, items for which many collectors will readily bid—and often bid high—in order to fill gaps in their specialised collections. Some countries have been particularly active in this field; others have a marked dislike of portraying members of their royal family on such mundane objects as matchboxes. Of the great variety of royalty labels issued over the years, many are now extremely scarce, not only because of the keen demand but because they were either limited printings or circulated for only a limited period.

The most famous, and probably the most popular, of all such labels are those familiarly known among collectors as 'the Dutch royalties'. Holland has always been the country most enthusiastic about portraying its beloved royal family on matchbox labels and some of these are now exceptionally rare. There were actually about 350 different varieties issued. One of the rarest is an untitled label which could easily be overlooked as not being a royalty one at all, since there is only one clue to its 'royal standing', a clue which could mean anything or nothing. The label shows the late Queen Wilhelmina of the Netherlands as a young child standing beside her favourite pony. The drawing is modestly printed in sepia on a beige background and the only indication of the child's identity is the border—narrow bands of red, white and blue. The Dutch royalty labels have ranged through all stages in the life of Queen Wilhelmina (who some years before her death renounced her title of Queen in favour of her daughter, then Princess Juliana). In most cases head-and-shoulder portraits were used, and she is shown as a young girl, a happy fiancée, a young matron, a middle-aged matron, and later, in her declining years, as a still regal though widowed queen.

The former Eindhoven Match Factory was the main producer of the Dutch royalty labels and great care was put into their preparation and printing. Every detail was correct, down to the pieces of jewellery worn by the Queen in some of her portraits, and in none is her likeness in any way distorted or grotesque—which cannot be said of numbers of less carefully produced royalty labels from other countries.

1 & 2. Famous Dutch royalty labels showing late Queen Wilhelmina 3. Austrian, c1900 4. Another in the Austrian set of 6 kings in Europe

1 & 2. Two Austrian labels issued at the beginning of the 20th century 3. King Christian X of Denmark 4. Old glazed Austrian label 5. King George V, Queen Mary and their sons and daughters on a Swedish label 6. King George V 7 & 8. King Edward VII and Queen Alexandra on a pair of glazed Austrian labels 9. The Duke of Windsor when Prince of Wales, Italian 10. Queen Wilhelmina of Holland on a Swedish label 11. Delhi Durbar commemorative showing King George V 12. Queen Wilhelmina of the Netherlands and her husband at the time of their marriage

Austria at the turn of the century was another great producer of royalty labels; some were excellent, some not so good. A set of five entitled 'Royal Scions' showed portrait drawings of the children of King George V and Queen Mary of Great Britain, and what is particularly striking to British collectors today is the strong resemblance between Prince Albert (later George VI, and here shown in Royal Navy midshipman's uniform) and the present young Prince Charles. Queen Helena of Italy and King Carol I of Rumania appeared on others. Scarce today is the single glazed label showing Kaiser Wilhelm I and called 'The Emperor of Germany'. Quite a number of the Austrian royalty labels were glazed, and these were usually good likenesses. Particularly good are a pair in full colour showing King Edward VII of Great Britain and his wife Queen Alexandra. Czechoslovakia also depicted King Edward and Queen Alexandra on several labels, but the representations are not good. In fact, one Czechoslovakian label with the inscription 'God Save King Edward VII and Queen Alexandra' is positively grotesque in its portrayal of the Queen—the drawing could be mistaken at first glance for that of a young boy.

One of the advantages of royalty labels is that they are usually easy to date, having been issued at the time a monarch was on the throne, or at least during his or her lifetime. Some commemorate special events during a reign, such as the Japanese 'Durbar Safety Match', with crudely produced drawings of King Edward and Queen Alexandra, issued at the time of their coronation as Emperor and Empress of India. This royal couple were particularly popular as label subjects, Sweden having also so honoured them on several occasions.

In more modern times royal personages have featured far less frequently, partly because their ranks are dwindling—they have thinned considerably during the past few years—and partly because fashion in labels has changed.

One comparatively modern issue which caused something of a furore in the early 1930s was a label entitled 'Smiling Prince' and showing an attractive photograph of the then Prince of Wales (now Duke of Windsor). The label gave

1

2

3

4

1. Very rare Dutch label; Queen Wilhelmina as a child 2. Swedish label showing Dutch Queen Wilhelmina as a young woman 3 & 4. King Edward VII and Queen Alexandra of Britain shown on a pair of labels from Czechoslovakia during their reign

no hint as to its country of origin but it was actually an Italian product commissioned by the owner of a successful bar in Malta. At the time protests were made at a member of the royal family being exploited to publicise a bar, although in fairness to the bar owner he had no advertising material whatever on the label. Even a diplomatic protest was made, but the boxes went into circulation and some have survived to this day. The label is now classed as scarce, especially if in used condition, because there was a rumour a few years ago that a reprint had been made; this was never proved, however, and there is nothing definite to indicate that mint labels in some collections were not produced at the time when they were put on sale in Malta.

One of the most popular of all Danish labels, both with the buying public and with collectors, was that which portrayed the well-loved King Christian X of Denmark. Dignified in design and well-printed, it shows an excellent etched likeness.

Young collectors have missed the heyday of the royalty label, but older collectors treasure their prizes like gold dust—there will be few new issues to join them.

1. Glazed Japanese label showing King Edward VII 2. King Edward VII and Queen Alexandra of Britain on a Swedish label 3. The same couple on a label from Czechoslovakia; here the portraits, especially of the Queen, are poor 4. The same royal couple as portrayed by Japan 5. Great Britain, pre-1939 6. King George V and Queen Mary of Britain on a Czechoslovakian label

14 Sport

WITH SPORT so much to the forefront these days in almost every country, the subject is likely to attract the attention of the matchbox-label designers and match manufacturers. Any label depicting one of the popular sports is off to a head start today as far as the consumer market is concerned; and every sport is catered for, from hunting to basketball, soccer to sand-yachting.

The early British manufacturers often displayed a sense of humour which would hardly seem commensurate with the staider times in which they lived. As remarked in earlier chapters, the late nineteenth and early twentieth centuries were the heyday of the pun, and a play on words formed the basis of many simple jokes. One of the most famous of the punning labels is Collard & Co's 'Cricket Match' which, printed in black on white paper, shows on one panel a drawing of the insect of the genus *Acheta* (better known as the cricket) whilst on the other panel an old-time batsman is about to take a swipe at the ball.

Another old British label was 'Royal Hunt Matches' with a grim-looking huntsman on the front panel and a panting stag on the reverse; a design which would probably raise cries of protest if it were issued today. 'Royal Hunt Matches' were originally marketed by J. H. Hunt & Co of Stratford, London, before it was taken over by larger concerns, and contemporary writings suggest that the huntsman was a portrait of Hunt himself. But investigations suggest that Hunt was actually a mild little man who let the rumour flourish merely because it amused him and fooled his rivals. To many collectors these old labels are hard to beat, despite the modern advantages of multi-colour printing, 'novelty' paper and other innovations.

1. From a long set of Mexican all-round labels depicting bullfighting 2. Red, white and blue American label showing basketball 3. Weightlifting in a recent sports set from Russia 4. The sprinter, from America

1

2

3

1. Label for an American football team 2. One of the world's most famous horse races 3. An American skillet, from set of 10 showing different sports

Hunting has featured in more recent times on issues from among other places, Sweden and Canada. The Swedish 'Sports' set of the late 1930s depicts twelve different sports and like most modern Swedish labels is well-printed. The Canadian offering is a skillet which, under the title of 'Club Matches', shows a huntsman putting his horse at a jump and has a frieze of three foxhounds, while at the same time it acts as an advertisement for Loblaw's—'Canada's finest foods of quality'.

The most comprehensive of all sports sets, in that it depicts the greatest number of different sports, was that issued in Australia to commemorate the holding of the Olympic Games there in 1956. Comprising 64 labels it had scope to be thorough. A modern set of Ohio 'Blue Tip' decorative boxes from the Ohio Match Co of USA includes tennis and skiing among its designs. American matchbox labels are very sport-conscious, and a wide variety have appeared. Very popular are those issued to honour American football teams, such as 'Golden Eagle Safety Matches'. The famous Kentucky Derby horse-race features on another American label with a drawing of the head of a racehorse, whilst the 'All American Safety Match' manufactured and distributed by the Capitol Safety Match Corporation is a patriotic design in red, white and blue of a football player kicking high.

Judo, the Japanese national sport, has featured on a modern set of labels from that country: simple but descriptive drawings showing no less than thirty-two different judo holds. Judo is the modern form of ju-jitsu and a combination of the most effective techniques of several schools of the old ju-jitsu. It is very Japanese—and so are the labels.

Russia is another country which issues sports labels in great quantity. A recent set of nine entitled 'Healthy Sport', which comes in several different combinations of colour, includes the only label the writer can recall as showing weight-lifting. No less energetic and requiring a high degree of skill is basketball, and it falls to Macao (that oft-disputed Portuguese possession on the mainland of China) to provide the most effective basketball label; it subtly incorporates an advertisement for the Eng Kee Go Tao basket-ball ground. Incidentally, despite the colourful labels and the high-sounding advertisements, matches made in Macao are reputed to be of poor quality. Made by 'sweated labour', mainly women, paid extremely low wages, they are unpredictable in performance: either they do not strike at all or else they flare dangerously and unexpectedly, or the heads fall off altogether; yet, being so ridiculously cheap, they far outsell matches made in Hong Kong or elsewhere in the area.

Soccer has a great following in Spain at present, and a few years ago the Spanish match firm Fosforera Espanola SA hit the jackpot with a long set of small-size labels for the typical small

1. Scarce old British label 2. Football from Deccan 3. One of a set from Portugal featuring badges of Portuguese football clubs 4. Old British all-round label of the 19th century

1. Modern Canadian skillet 2. From the Swedish sports set of the 1940s 3. From set of 12 sports labels from Czechoslovakia 4. Italian export label 5. Italian for export to Malta 6. From the modern set of 32 Japanese judo labels 7. Mexican boxers on a 1930s set from Mexico 8. American label of the 1930s 9. Macao features volleyball on a modern label

Spanish slide-tray boxes. These illustrated the crests of well-known Spanish football clubs, including such world-renowned favourites as Real Madrid. All the small boys as well as adults frenziedly gathered the labels to complete sets, whether or not they had any interest in matchbox labels as such (and it is unlikely that they did have any interest in that direction, as there are few label collectors in Spain). Hasty reprints were rushed through again and again and it must have been one of the biggest booms in match sales which the industry has known.

Spanish-speaking Mexico also does a brisk trade in boxes of matches featuring sporting subjects. The 'Mariposa' (Butterfly) brand of some years back featured photographs of popular Mexican boxers on the reverse panels; it was successful in effectively presenting them in somewhat unconventional poses in a sport where this is difficult.

The Mexican 'Deportistas' sets of all-round labels for spring-flap boxes in different sizes have beautifully-produced full-colour 'action' pictures of various sports. One of the sets is devoted entirely to well-proportioned young women taking part, very decoratively, in a selection of sports. But of course it is the bullfighting labels which really sell matches in Mexico. Dozens of very long sets—some comprising as many as 95 labels—have been issued over the years, many of them of splendid quality, with naturally-coloured, beautiful drawings or good photographs, and glazed. Every move in the matador's art has been faithfully reproduced and one set depicts the life of the bulls from the time they are reared on the plains until they die in the ring. The subject is a controversial one in some countries, but Mexico knows how to exploit its glamour.

The 1957 Indian issue called 'Fotbol', with a picture of a player in action, had a short life and a merry one, for someone must have pointed out the spelling mistake to the manufacturer and he, perhaps in umbrage, did not issue any more! Unfortunately it has been impossible to locate a copy now for illustration in this volume.

Among the more unusual sports used on labels comes the Mexican national game *jai alai*, very fast, played with a hard ball on a *fronton* or court, the participants handling the ball in curved baskets strapped to their wrists. Its European equivalent is the Basque game *pelota*, which employs a somewhat similar 'racquet'. *Jai alai* is featured on a modern Japanese label.

With cycling such a popular sport in Belgium it is not surprising that there are several sets of Belgian matchbox labels featuring well-known cyclists, usually the road-racing idols who take part in the classic long-distance races such as the gruelling Tour de France.

15 *Transport*

THE STUDENT of transport looking for an illustration of some particular type of vehicle might do well by turning to matchbox labels, because from the Roman chariot to the jet aircraft means of getting about have fascinated label designers.

The chariot must be one of the earliest forms of wheeled transport one could depict, and Poland selected it for 'Chariot Safety Matches' with the design of a Roman gentleman driving his 'equipage' at full speed. Another early, though less ancient, form of transport is the ice boat, a strange-looking contraption designed for skimming over the ice. In such countries as Holland which have large stretches of ice in the wintertime, ice boats were (and sometimes still are) in frequent use; a cross-bar with a 'skate' at each end shapes the craft. The former match factory at Eindhoven in Holland issued 'The Ice Boat Paraffin Match' at the beginning of this century, with a clear illustration of a boat in action.

Matchbox labels can in fact be quite instructive about craft from other countries. For instance, 'The Dhow'; this was a brand issued by WIMCO of India for Arab countries and was first put on sale in Aden. It is a pretty little label and merits a place in any collection, although later printings were not always so good in quality. The dhow is a native trading vessel with

1

2

3

4

5

6

7

8

9

10

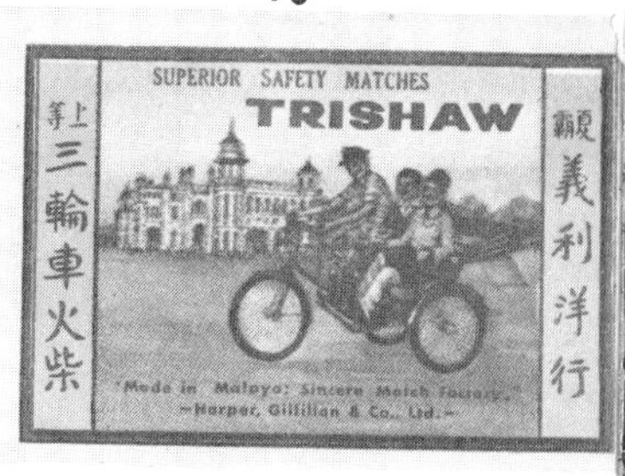

11

12

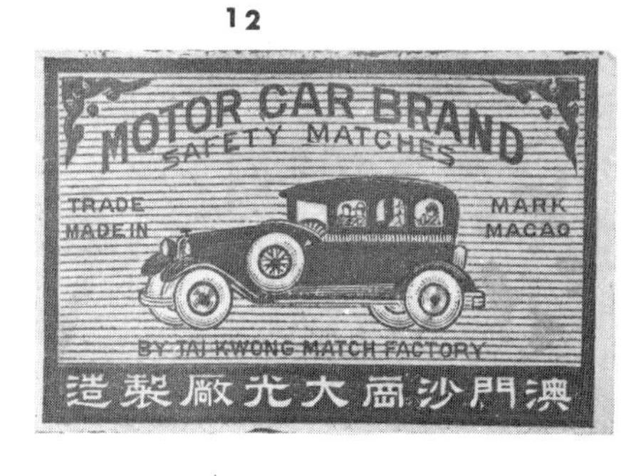

13

1. Japanese shipping label 2. Modern advertising label 3. From a Danish set, c1960 4. One from the recent Australian set of 64 veteran cars 5. Scarce old Dutch label 6. From a modern Dutch set depicting motor cycles 7. For a Belgian 20-match miniature box 8 & 9. Two Brazilian labels in the size most favoured in that country 10. Oriental transport from Malaya 11. Swedish label for a Swiss airline 12. The type of car dates this one from Macao 13. Malayan label pre-1939

1. From the Finnish ships set of the 1960s 2. Early Swedish label for export to the East Indies 3. Indian label 4. Old Swedish label 5. Indian 6. Dingee, an East Indian ferryboat, shown on an Indian label

ne mast, a very long yard and a lateen sail, and is used on the Arabian Sea. The name was formerly given especially to such vessels used in the slave trade.

In Egypt, the felucca is equally familiar and although classed as a vessel used in the Mediterranean it is predominantly in use on the Nile; the very long yard enables the sails to catch every breath of air when the vessel is negotiating arrow stretches of the river, where palm trees se on both sides and the only noticeable current f wind is above their tops. A felucca can be ropelled by sails, oars or both. A somewhat ylised and not very clear drawing of a felucca ppears on the Egyptian 'El Felouqua' label.

In Malta one may see the dghajsa, the port's maid-of-all-work; another oar-propelled vessel. In 1950 a label entitled 'Maltese Dghajsa' caused quite a stir in the island. The boxes of 50 matches suddenly appeared on sale almost everywhere there, but were found to be of poor quality and gave off unpleasant fumes when struck. The one operating match firm in Malta raised loud protests on receiving complaints about the matches, because it had not manufactured them and felt it was being given a bad name. To add to the annoyance of the consumers the vessel was shown with two sails, whereas the dghajsa is oar-propelled and is really an elegantly-designed little craft. A lot of noise was created by everyone except the erring manufacturer, who diplomatically maintained complete silence, and it was finally decided (probably in order to close the matter) that the matches came from Italy. However no match firm in Italy has ever confirmed or denied this! Fortunately the brand was short-lived—and that made the labels a good item for collectors.

Most of the large shipping lines and a great many smaller ones have at one time or another had their own matchbox labels. Boxes of matches are now largely being superseded here by book matches, but quite a number of collectors specialise in shipping labels and are able to build very worthwhile collections. Up to the late 1930s Bryant & May had something of the monopoly of these labels in Britain and 'B. & M. Shipping' is a group of labels over which many collectors enthuse. All-round-the-box labels, they had the famous Bryant & May ark design on the front panel, and the reverse panel bore a coloured picture of the ship in which they were to be distributed. The boxes were given away free at the ships' bars, and some of the earlier types have 'Matches Not for Sale' printed in red letters along the front panel.

Shipping companies of course usually carry matches manufactured in their own country or area of the world, and the design is usually a picture of the vessel and/or the house flag. Some are all-round-the-box, some are single labels. Some come in sets, such as those issued ten years ago by the Zim Line of Israel, with several designs to a set. Others count as sets by being different labels issued for all the ships in a particular fleet, as with the Ben Line issues for its various vessels.

Lovers of the internal-combustion engine are well catered for on labels, motor cars of various types from the early vintage models to the latest racing giants having been pictured by many different countries. The interest which has grown

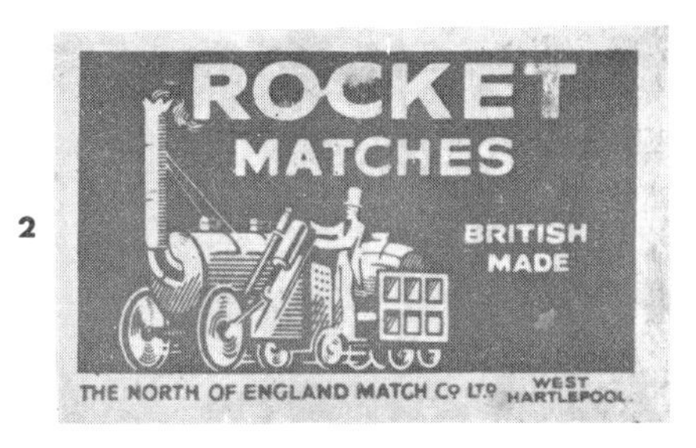

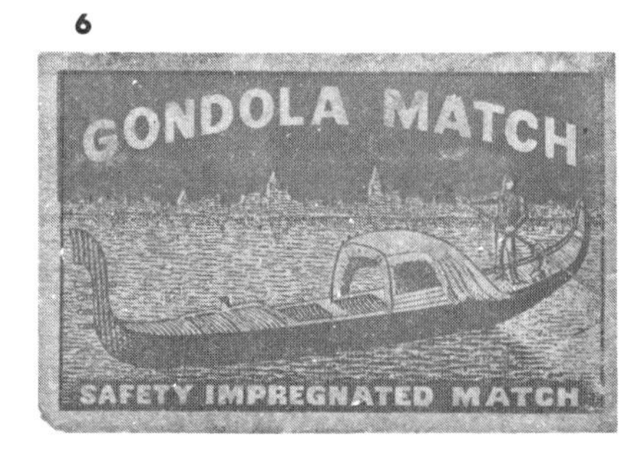

1. Scarce old Belgian label 2. Blue and white single box label from the North of England 3. Old Austrian 4. Czechoslovakian label for the Sudan Railways 5. Label issued by a famous shipping line 6. Old label giving no clue to its country of origin 7. Portuguese label advertising a Scandinavian airline 8. Rare label for matches distributed only in a famous American trans-continental train

in the last few years in vintage and veteran cars has promoted several manufacturers to issue long sets. Australia's set of 64 'Vintage Cars' proved a great draw for collectors all over the world, and British-made matches were contained in boxes with all-round labels advertising the VG grocery supermarket chain on the front panels and a series of drawings of vintage cars on the reverse.

Czechoslovakia has weighed in with a set of 10 'Automobiles 1897-1957', the sets each containing ten labels of bicycles, motor cycles and scooters. Such labels as this appeal to the motoring enthusiast as well as the label collector and are therefore a good source of revenue to match manufacturers.

The Mauritius Match Manufacturing Co Ltd, on its 'The Norge Safety Matches', first put on the export market in 1925, showed a picture of an airship flying above mountain peaks. The airship, after which the matches were named, is the one which took an Italian polar expedition, headed by General Nobile, on an ill-fated attempt to reach the North Pole. The airship was

1

2

3

4

5

6

7

8

9

1 & 2. Two old Austrian labels 3. Polish export label 4. Egyptian, showing the sailing vessel of the Nile 5. Russian airline label 6. Issued in India long before catamarans became popular elsewhere 7. An early submarine shown on an old Belgian label 8. Italian, c1946 9. Ceylon

lost but the gallant attempt so stirred the imagination of the public at the time that the label was expected to have a ready sale.

Titles given to matchbox labels are sometimes grandiose for what they show. 'The Lamm's Sub-Marine Brand' from Belgium in the early 1920s leads one to expect a picture of some impressive craft, but actually shows a man standing on what appears to be a torpedo with a flagstaff poking out of a hole at the top. No doubt this label *did* reasonably faithfully reproduce a picture of an early submarine, but it looks ludi-

1. Scarce old Dutch label 2. Controversial label from Malta 3. Czechoslovakian label publicising the country's railways 4. One of a set of all-round British labels for a supermarket chain 5. Mauritius featured an ill-fated airship 6. Indian 7. Japanese shipping line label 8. Indian brand 9. Mauritius

crous today!

'Catamaran' is a title which conjures up visions of the rather strange-looking double-hulled craft fashionable among sailing enthusiasts today, but the Indian 'Catamaran' label shows three men fishing from the type of raft or float used as a surf-boat in the East and West Indies. The picture clearly shows the vessel's high prow, designed to assist it in riding the surf.

The now-vanished North of England Match Co's most popular brand was its 'Rocket' Matches. The design was of George Stephenson's famous steam engine, the first to run on the Stockton & Darlington Railway. The matches were sold only in the north of England and with Stephenson's historic north country connections they were best-sellers for many years. All-round-the-box labels were mainly produced, but there is also a single box label printed in blue and white. The North of England Match Co Ltd ceased trading in 1954 after a disastrous fire which gutted its premises.

Another old form of transport shown on a label was the trolley car. 'The Trolley Car Safety Match' was produced in Austria in the early 1900s, intended for export to the United States. The vehicle concerned has long ago departed from the scene, except in one place—the modern city of San Francisco, California, USA. There trolley-cars similar to the one depicted on the label still ply on a regular service, proving adept at negotiating the steep hills which are such a characteristic of the city. They are well patronised and are a great attraction to tourists.

Trains, naturally, have featured prominently on matchbox labels although they are now rather out of fashion as label subjects as air travel takes over even for the bulk of the internal services in some countries. Sweden's 'Protection from Fire Safety Matches' of the early 1900s showed a railway engine of the period, whilst Ceylon's 'Special Train' resembles the famous steam engines which pulled the expresses on Britain's railways before the diesel age. The Broadway Limited, which belonged to the old 'romantic' era of the American railways and which ran between Chicago and New York, gave its Pullman passengers its own special label—an attractive one in natural colours showing the train speeding on its long journeys.

Motor cycle, jeep, bicycle, seaplane, subway car, raft, gondola, racing car, have all found their way on to matchbox labels at one time and another; with such a wide variety of subjects, transport labels are a favourite speciality for collectors.

Appendix

PERFECTION
SOLO MATCH WORKS
MADE IN CZECHOSLOVAKIA

2—CHICHEN ITZA, YUC.

M. IND. REG. NUM.
CIA. MEXICANA DE CERILLOS Y FOSFOROS, S.A.
GERANIO 98.—MEXICO, D.F.
PERM. N. I D.F. HECHO EN MEXICO. REG. HDA. Nº 1.
30 LUCES

VIAJEROS
LA IMPERIAL
MEXICO, D. F.

Appendix

I: Clubs

The British Matchbox Label & Booklet Society (Hon Sec: Mr J. H. Luker, 283/285 Worplesdon Road, Guildford, Surrey, England) caters for collectors of labels *and* bookmatch covers throughout the world. Formed in 1945, it is the largest society of its kind in the world and is fully international in membership. It issues a printed magazine six times a year, holds an annual exhibition in London and several rallies in different parts of England through the year, and also offers many services to collectors.

The West & Midlands Match Label Club (Hon Sec: Mr F. C. Oakley, 67 West Park Avenue, Northfield, Birmingham 31, England) draws most of its members from the Midlands and the Gloucester and Bristol areas of England. It issues a duplicated magazine several times a year and holds an annual exhibition in a different Midlands town each year.

There are several smaller clubs with a purely local membership, for instance the Norwich Phillumenist Society, which has been in existence for ten years. These hold regular meetings in their home towns. Some are affiliated to the British Matchbox Label & Booklet Society.

The Australian Match Cover Collectors' Society is the main body for Australasia (Hon Sec: Mr T. R. Anthony, 88 Essex Street, Footscray West, 3012, Victoria, Australia). It issues a club magazine regularly.

For collectors in India and neighbouring countries, the recently-formed Indian Matchbox Label Association can be very helpful (Hon Sec: Mr L. N. Das, c/o Maj-Gen C. N. Das, E-in-C's Branch, Kashmir House, New Delhi -11, India). It issues a duplicated magazine devoted mainly to labels from the Indian sub-continent and offers Indian labels for sale at special concession prices for its members.

In the USA, there are no clubs for collectors of matchbox labels operating at present, although there are several organisations catering for collectors of book-match covers. There is, however, a growing interest in matchbox labels and it is hoped that some enterprising collectors will soon band together. A number of US collectors are members of the British Matchbox Label & Booklet Society.

There are local clubs in many countries, notably in Belgium, Czechoslovakia, Germany, Portugal and Russia, and all hold meetings, social get-togethers and exhibitions for their members. Some, especially in Czechoslovakia where there are a great many label collectors, invite guests from other countries to exhibit at their annual exhibitions.

II: Prices

The pricing of matchbox labels is difficult. There is no official label catalogue, although several people have from time to time drawn up catalogues of their own, and prices paid depend mainly on the enthusiasm of individual collectors for particular items. For instance, a collector may be willing to pay several shillings for a 'Rose of Peckham' label because he is called Rose and lives in Peckham, whereas another collector would pay no more than 2d for the same one. A US collector whose father was stationed at Camp Stuart during world war II may be prepared to give a substantial sum for one of the Camp Stuart all-round labels which were available to wartime servicemen in the camp, although the intrinsic value of the label may not be more than 2s 6d at most, perhaps much less to the average collector.

Generally speaking, old Austrian glazed labels (Royalty, Maharajahs, etc) fetch up to 2s each; modern Australian set labels (Flora, Fauna, Mythology, etc) 3d to 6d each according to whether sold in sets or singly. Spanish inserts change hands nowadays at about 2s each, sometimes more if people are anxious to get particular ones to complete sets. Old British ('The Merton Monster', Braided Cigar Lights, etc) between 20s and 60s each, although some really old and very rare complete boxes, or even labels only, may fetch up to 100s or 120s each. Modern Czechoslovakian sets (with which the market is usually flooded, as a great many different sets are issued every year) range from about 10d to 2s 6d per set; current labels from sets ('Camp' flags, 'Old Cornish Mine', etc) 2d to 3d each; current advertising labels are usually the cheapest and range from 1d each. Modern Russian sets (issued in great quantity) can usually be bought quite cheaply and are a colourful addition to the album.

As a rough guide to the sums paid for labels in recent years, here is a list of some of the prices realised for items offered for auction at rallies of the British Matchbox Label & Booklet Society. These give a fair indication of likely market values, although the occasional item rockets way above what might have been expected, usually because someone is determined to have it for one reason or another.

The highest price ever paid for a single label at one of these auctions was £32—for a copy of the John Walker label, the first printed label for friction matches.

Other prices realised over the past few years include the following:

3 Queen Wilhelmina 'Dutch Royalty' labels 12s 6d
The 'Adam & Eve' label 16s
'Red Cross' label (Norway) 10s 6d
Box, complete with matches, W. Barber's 'Royal Scented Fusees' ... 130s
Box, complete with matches, Martin Harris's 'Royal British Matches' 65s
'Punch' set of 30 Scout emblems 11s
15 'Tower Bridge' labels, variations (Belgium) 20s
Set of 49 'Bullfighter' labels (Mexico) 22s 6d
First Bryant & May safety box & outer wrapper, issued 1862 ... 100s
Used set 'Army Badges' labels (Australia) 22s 6d
Ditto, mint condition 10s
Royal visit to Canada commemorative matchbox, 1959 ... ... 6s 6d
'Red Cross' sulphur label (Sweden) 28s
2 rare modern boxes complete with matches (Albania) 25s
The 'Erin go Bragh' label (Ireland) 10s
'Jesus Christ' label (Japan) 15s
'Merton Monster', all-round label (GB) 18s
'Nurse Cavell' box and packet labels 70s
4 from the set of 5 US 'De Luxe' birds (the fifth label was a very limited printing and is virtually unobtainable) 25s
2 'England's Glory' all-round labels advertising local regattas ... 8s
The 'Johnstown Flood City' label (USA) 5s 6d
4 old Bryant & May labels showing Eastern scenes 100s

Here are some individual pricings. They represent the prices I would be willing to pay if I wanted the items listed.

'The Canary' label (Flanders) ... 3s 6d

'Platypus' label (Australia) ... 5s

'I shall return' label (USA) ... 10s

Propaganda label of world war II (Japan) ... 7s 6d

Costumes set, purple background, set of 12 (Sweden) ... 10s

Ballet dancers, set of 16 (Russia) ... 7s 6d

Complete box Bougies de Poche (candle matches) ... 15s

'General Gordon' label (Sweden) ... 7s 6d

Royal Visit to Canada skillet (1959) ... 4s

'The Abyssinian' labels (Sweden) ... 1s

'The Antediluvian Iguanadon' label (Belgium) ... 5s

'God Save King Edward & Queen Alexandra' label (Czechoslovakia) 1s 6d

'Greyhound' label (USA) ... 4s 6d

'Fear God' label (India) ... 10s

'Copperhead' label (USA) ... 1s

'Don't Talk About Ships' label, yellow paper (S Africa) ... 3s 6d

Ditto, blue paper ... 10s

'Dunyerbit' labels (several varieties) ... 2s each

'Bunker Hill' label (USA) ... 1s

'Cabot' label (GB) ... 15s

'Capt Webb' label, as illustrated (GB) ... 15s

'Rulers of the World' set of 5 labels, used (Mexico) ... 15s

'Admiral Brand' label (Norway) ... 3s 6d

'Shirley Temple' label (Iran) ... 2s 6d

'Imperial Topical Match' label (GB) ... 100s

Some collectors may not agree with these valuations, the pricing of labels being, as explained, a very personal thing. But for this list I have set aside personal preferences, basing the valuations on thirty-eight years' collecting experience, during which time many thousands of labels of all types have passed through my hands.

Also it must be remembered that a great many labels come in a number of variations—perhaps just two, or in some cases over a hundred—and whilst one variety may be common and worth only a few pence, another variety of the same label may be extremely uncommon and worth up to a few pounds. An example of this is the wartime South African 'Don't Talk About Ships' propaganda label; the black printing on yellow paper variety was produced in quite large quantities and many examples have survived, being worth, at the most, 3s 6d; but the variety printed in black on *dark blue* paper was a very limited issue and the price for one of these could start at 10s and probably rise easily to over £1 sterling.

I have stated earlier that old Austrian glazed labels usually change hands at about 2s each, yet I have recently seen them offered for sale at 5s each. I would not pay that myself, but another collector, wanting specific sets or a single label to complete a set, might be perfectly willing to do so. Over the past few years the prices of labels, particularly of the earlier varieties, have risen sharply, as more and more people have taken up collecting. This tends to make collectors of long standing feel that prices are becoming inflated, because we can remember buying for a few pence a label for which a newer collector must pay several shillings.

Prices are always based on labels in good condition. This is important: the value of any label drops steeply if it is torn, dirty, rubbed or otherwise defaced. All-round labels which have been cut (ie are not complete with all panels) are completely valueless, no matter how old or uncommon. In some cases used labels cost more than mint copies, but this is something which the collector will learn with experience. In the case of old labels, much depends on whether manufacturers made stocks of 'remainders' available; in modern labels it usually hinges on whether or not manufacturers make mint labels available at all, some being very strict about not doing so. 'Fashions' in labels also cause prices to fluctuate and the types most sought after one year may be out of favour the next year, but this usually applies to modern labels rather than the old 'classics'.

The beginner is advised not to pay high prices for labels at first, but to start by building a collection of current brands, labels obtained through exchange with other collectors and perhaps some reasonably-priced sets bought through a reputable source such as the Label Pool or Approval Service run by the British Matchbox Label & Booklet Society. The society offers excellent value for beginners in mixed packets of labels costing 1s for 30, 3s for 100 and so on (prices correct at time of going to press). Or better-class labels, priced singly or in sets, can be had on approval by Society members.

There are of course such things as forgeries, so, as with all collecting hobbies, the golden rule is not to buy anything expensive until you know and understand what you are buying.

Acknowledgments

IN SELECTING the labels to be described and illustrated in this book we have obviously been able only to skim the surface of the vast numbers which have been issued over the years, and which still continue to pour from the printing presses, and we thank all those persons who offered suggestions for labels to be included and/or offered the loan of such items. It is regretted that it was not possible to use them all, but everyone's interest was much appreciated.

Special thanks are due to Mr Douglas S. Blake and Mr Frederick Bundy for the loan of labels from the groups in which they specialise, to Mr Gordon Appleby for assisting with Russian translations and to Mr Lalit Das for providing background information on Indian mythology.

JOAN RENDELL

Index

© 1963 ASSOCIATED MATCH COS INC N.Y.
JAPAN

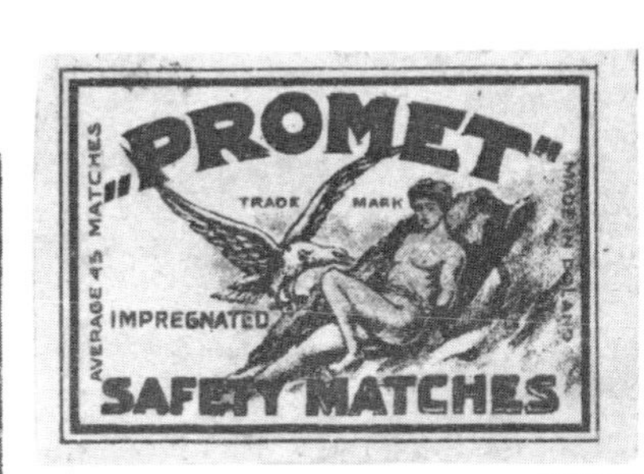
„PROMET"
TRADE MARK
AVERAGE 45 MATCHES
MADE IN POLAND
IMPREGNATED
SAFETY MATCHES

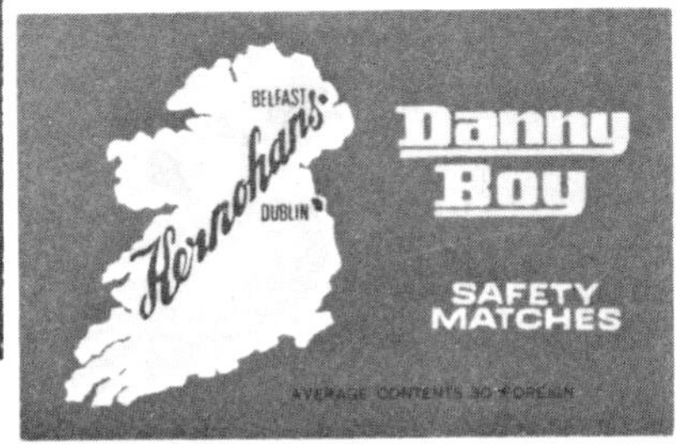
BELFAST
Kernohan's
DUBLIN
Danny Boy
SAFETY MATCHES

THE MARTELLO
FINEST QUALITY
EASY STRIKE
SAFETY MATCH
MADE IN BELGIUM

HUMBER

MULILO-FIRE
TRADE MARK
SAFETY MATCHES
AFRICAN MATCH CO. LTD.
MADE IN ZAMBIA

THREE SURFERS
MADE BY THE SAVO FACTORY, FINLAND
IMPREGNATED
SAFETY MATCHES

Getaway people get SUPER NATIONAL!
National
AVERAGE 33 FOREIGN MATCHES · 2d

MOONRAKER
SAFETY MATCHES
FOREIGN MADE
AVERAGE 30 CONTENTS
SOLE DISTRIBUTOR
H. J. GOODEY, SWINDON

SAFETY MATCHES
TRADE MARK
MADE IN YUGOSLAVIA
IMPREGNATED

FOUR HORSE BRAND

PRICE
RE 0-0-6
SAFETY MATCHES

PANORAMA
CONTENTS 30 FOREIGN
DAMP PROOF
DOVER
IMPREGNATED
SAFETY MATCHES
FOLKESTONE
MARGATE

CANTON

CRANBROOK MILL
Series of 10—No. 2
FINEST QUALITY – MADE IN FINLAND
AVERAGE CONTENTS 34 DAMP PROOF STICKS
THE KENTISH MATCH CO., SIDCUP

103
S. IV/1
Bescheidenheit fesselt.
Neueste kleine Blumensprache

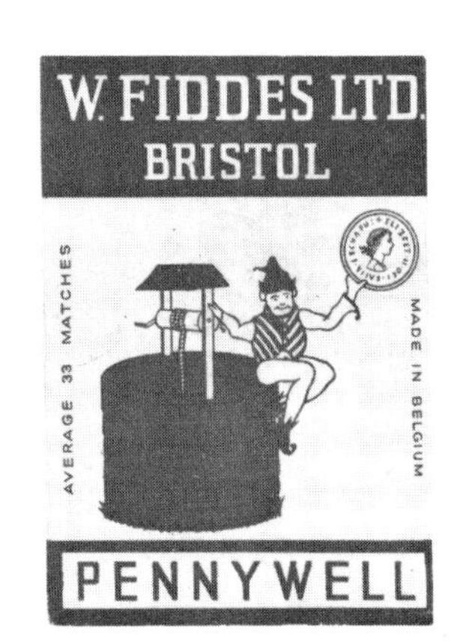
W. FIDDES LTD.
BRISTOL
AVERAGE 33 MATCHES
MADE IN BELGIUM
PENNYWELL

19
REWE IN DER EUROGROUP
REWE
Schmunzelwitz No. 0068

138
33

SEP 200